The MUSIC of CREATiON

EXPLORING VERSE AND VIBRATION IN THE BIBLE

A Mystic Pagan Guide by

JANET RUDOLPH

FOREWORD BY PAUL ROBEAR
PRESIDENT/EXECUTIVE DIRECTOR, CUYUMUNGUE INSTITUTE

Artist's Statement by Susan Tapia Leon

DANCE SPIRIT
Acrylic, 2020

Whispering energy . . .
Moving our heart into a spiral dance
Dance since the beginning!
Dancing at the echo of Great Mystery.
Manifesting always in silent movement, dancing,
Evolving, renewing, transforming each cell of our body.
Getting lost
Getting found
Swirling, pending
Trusting greater manifestation of endless love!

Susana Tapia Leon is an elder native of the Andes of Ecuador.
Midwife for the process of life. She travels across communities
sharing music, voice, healing, art in life.

"Janet Rudolph is an outlaw scholar of the best kind."
Rachel Pollack
Award-winning author of 41 books, including *78 Degrees of Wisdom*, *Unquenchable Fire* and the creator of The Shining Tribe tarot deck.

Advance praise for
The Music of Creation

Rudolph's retranslations of the bible and the experiential exercises that bring their vibrancy into our bodies, hearts, minds, and soul transform our perception of our world and open doors between our human, everyday realm of existence and that of spirit and divinity. Each section of *The Music of Creation* is so packed full of new panoramic understandings of divinity, humanity, mystery, and more that most could be a book in themselves. This is a work that should be discussed widely among scholars, clergy, shamans, and other spiritual practitioners for years to come, but will also be deeply meaningful and revolutionary to anyone who wishes to interact more profoundly with the Hebrew Bible. Read this book and find that your beliefs about yourself, Divinity, the universe in all its energetic glory, and your place in it have been unfurled in ways you could never have imagined.

Carolyn Lee Boyd
Author of *The Temple of the Subway Goddess*

In *The Music of Creation*, scholar and mystic Janet Rudolph invites her readers not only to ponder the origins of sacred language and chant but to become part of it, or to recognize that we already are. She takes us back to the roots of Hebrew scripture, guides us through the well-known and loved King James Version to her own Mystic Pagan Version, which models for us how to make meaning fresh and alive. Always she returns to the sound of the Hebrew syllables, encouraging us to find the music of creation in our own voice and breath, our own bodies, our own visionary understanding of timeless wisdom.

The Music of Creation speaks of Sacred Languages for which the sounds and words for divinity call in Divinity itself.

The Music of Creation is a rare book. Like most of Janet Rudolph's writing, it's part invocation, part scholarship and part playful practice. From the very first pages it invites you not only to read but to participate and let sound, gesture and image become your living companions, or avenues of exploration.

Rudolph leads us through ancient names and sacred texts with reverence and curiosity, unearthing hidden but surprising goddess aspects. Womb, breasts, umbilical cords are re-integrated in the great origin story. Her Mystic Pagan translation of ancient verses reads as sheer poetry and is worth its own prayer book… Elohim becomes All-Potential, YHVH a living vibration, and mudra, mantra and mandala are joined to create a full-bodied practice of manifestation. With a hermeneutic approach that feels both ancient and fresh, this book becomes an invitation to peel back the inherited translations of sacred texts and discover their shimmering layers of meaning, each revealing a new depth of resonance.

What I loved most is how inclusive this book feels. You need no prior knowledge of religion or sacred texts; you don't need to 'believe' in any of their premises. You do not need to be musical, or even confident in your voice, to enter and be moved by the chant. Instead, you are simply encouraged to experiment, linger on syllables, buzz like a honeybee, feel the energy move through your body and make it your own. Trees, hand postures and simple rituals anchor the practices in the natural world.

Just like sound itself, the book offers a multi-layered journey into the vibrational heart of creation, where mysticism, embodiment and contemporary insight meet. This is scholarship as sacred play, a weaving of the mystical and the practical.

At a time when many spiritual paths emphasize separation or perfection, *The Music of Creation* offers a paradigm of blending and harmony, a reminder that we are part of a living continuum, instead of outsiders looking in. Whether you are new to chanting or have been walking a sacred path for decades, this book will open portals of perception and return you to the joy, mystery and creativity that connect all things.

Eline Kieft, PhD
Author of *Dancing in the Muddy Temple: A Moving Spirituality of Land and Body* and founder of *Wild Soul Centre for Embodied Spirituality.*

PRAISE FOR OTHER BOOKS BY JANET RUDOLPH

Praise for
When Moses Was a Shaman

It is rare to read a book with as many "*aha!*" eureka moments as Janet Rudolph's fascinating and scholarly – yet accessible – *When Moses Was a Shaman.* Even if you're sure you are familiar with Moses, the Bible, Biblical legends, and world mythology, there will be something here to surprise you and give you food for thought. A shaman herself, Janet Rudolph shines historical, shamanic, and mythic spotlights on this pivotal and important figure. Highly recommended!

Judika Illes
Author of *Encyclopedia of Spirits, Encyclopedia of Mystics, Saints, and Sages*, and other books devoted to spirituality and the magical arts.

Praise for
When Eve Was a Goddess
A Shamanic View of the Bible

Reading *When Eve Was a Goddess* put me into a more spiritual frame of mind. I find myself looking at the world from a different perspective each time I read another section.

Rudolph has done impressive research. She relates stories from different religious traditions. There are insights into Hebrew letters, the role of seed in spreading both spiritual and physical traits, masculine versus feminine, for example. It's short, but should be read slowly, and pondered.

Susan Lerner
Author of *Children of Lies, A Suitable Husband, In the Middle of Almost and Other Stories*, and *The Journal Project: Capturing the magic of family life through stories.*

When Eve Was a Goddess provides a wonderful look into ancient legends, giving the reader alternate interpretations of Biblical stories. You will be swept up in the author's amalgam of scholarship and spirituality.

Alice Laby
Author of *The Secret War of Henry Rebbenoff*

Praise for
Desperately Seeking Persephone
The True Story of My Shamanic Journey
Through the Underworld

Desperately seeking, joyfully being found: Janet Rudolph takes us with her on a journey that is at once deeply personal to her and as well as mythic. In her story, interwoven with Persephone's and Inanna's, we may recognize elements of our own, find inspiration and companionship for our own quest and questions. Janet also reminds us that life is full of mysteries, time spirals backward and forward; we not only seek but we are also found by human angels who come into our lives when we most need them, and who are, in some way, always with us. This beautiful, thoughtful, funny, poetic memoir gives the reader comfort and inspires awe.

Elizabeth Cunningham
Award-winning author of The Maeve Chronicles, Over the Edge of the World, The Return of the Goddess, The Wild Mother, and others.

I absolutely loved *Desperately Seeking Persephone*. What a wonderful book - exciting, wise, heart-expanding, life-affirming. This is profoundly inspiring. Thank you, thank you!

Jocelyn Stevenson
Winner of the BAFTA Children's Awards Special Award for contribution to children's media. She's currently finishing two novels for 9–12-year-olds – The Waterubas. Children's television writings include Sesame Street, Fraggle Rock, and The Magic School Bus.

A SUFI STORY[1]

A Sufi initiate was walking along the shore of a lake when he heard chanting. He was enthralled and stopped to listen. Since he practiced his own chanting, he recognized this chant from his own teachers. He realized the chanter was not doing the chant correctly. He had heard that with the correct chanting, one could do miraculous things, such as walk on water, create an endless cornucopia of food, turn water into wine, heal wounds. He had not experienced any of this magic himself but as the diligent student he was, he resolved to find the chanter. He hoped to correct him so he, too, could partake in the miracles that were sure to come from this practice.

The student looked around and realized that the chanting was coming from an island in the middle of the lake. He would need a boat. The student walked until he found a fisherman coming in from his day's haul, arranged to borrow his boat, and took off for the island. When he arrived, he landed on a small beach. He pulled the boat up and began to listen for and look for the chanter. He had to climb a small hill. At the top there was small cabin with the door open. He peered in and saw a man standing, trembling, lost in trance, while doing the chant. The student waited patiently as the chanter did not notice him. Finally, the student yawned and sighed loudly. The chanter was startled out of his reverie.

"Oh my," he said, "I did not notice you there. Have you been here long? You are welcome, come inside and have some tea."

The student responded, "I don't have a lot of time, but I came to find you because I recognized the chant, and I realized you were doing it wrong. I wanted to help you. I understand you can do miraculous things with the correct chant."

"Oh, thank you," the chanter clapped his hands. "I am so delighted you have come."

---

[1] This story was told to me by one of my own teachers. I do not know its origins.

And with that the student explained how to do the chant correctly. The chanter listened and then practiced the correct way to do the chant.

He thanked the student and waved goodbye. The student made his way back down to his boat. On the way back, the student began thinking about this interaction and was proud of himself for helping out the poor chanter. He was about ½ way back to the other shore when he noticed the chanter run out of his hut in a hurry, rush down to the shore. The man continued running right over the top of the water and approached the student's boat. Standing above the student he said, "I am so glad I caught up to you. I was doing the chant just as you told me and then suddenly, I forgot and found myself chanting in my old way. I feared I was doing it wrong. Can you please tell me that correction again.?"

Table of Contents

FOREWORD

By Paul Robear
President / Executive Director
Cuyamungue Institute

In *The Music of Creation*, Janet Rudolph invites us into a deeply resonant exploration of sound, language, and the vibrational essence of the sacred. Drawing inspiration from Hebrew as a sacred language — alongside traditions that honor Sanskrit, Latin, and other power-syllable–based languages — she reimagines Biblical passages through the lenses of rational, symbolic, and mystical inquiry. What emerges is more than translation: it is a pathway into embodied experience.

Janet's *Mystic Pagan Version* of Biblical texts offers a refreshing perspective. By stripping away gendered language and returning to elemental roots, she reminds us that divinity is not bound by duality but woven into the rhythms of nature and the breath of the cosmos. Her work stands in conversation with pioneers like Neil Douglas-Klotz, yet she forges her own voice — one that blends scholarship with lived spirituality.

Perhaps most compelling is Janet's invitation into sacred play. The book does not simply present intellectual commentary; it opens a doorway into practice. Through chanting, experimenting with seed syllables, and engaging the vibrational essence of Hebrew words, she guides the reader into a visceral encounter with mystery. Whether one sings beautifully or chants imperfectly, the vibration itself becomes a bridge between heaven and earth, body and spirit, self and community.

As I read, I was touched by how Janet's vision parallels practices of the trance postures and embodied rituals of the Cuyamungue Institute. For over 50 years, following the pioneering work of anthropologist Dr. Felicitas D. Goodman, the practice of Ritual Postures has opened portals to ancestral wisdom and collective presence. Both approaches affirm that wisdom is not abstract but lived, accessible through the body as much as the mind.

The Music of Creation is both ancient and fresh — and groundbreaking. It honors lineage and tradition, yet it makes them accessible for today's seekers. It is a book for scholars, mystics, and explorers alike — for anyone who feels the call to listen more deeply to the music already humming through creation.

Introduction

The knower of the mystery of sound
knows the mystery of the whole universe.
Hazrat Inayat Khan[2]

Hebrew, like Latin and Sanskrit, is known as a sacred language. Sacred languages use power syllables to communicate. This means is that the words themselves carry a vibrational element that we, as human beings, find meaningful and compelling. In many, if not most cultures, words with especially strong vibrational energy are used to indicate God, Divinity or Creator. When such words are spoken or intoned, they have the effect of traveling along vibrational pathways connecting us to that which is grander than ourselves. In this manner they resonate within our bodies as well as throughout heaven and the earth.

The purpose of this book is to examine important Biblical passages from the Elder Bible [Hebrew Bible][3] and re-translate

---

[2] Hazrat Inayat Khan, *The Music of Life*, Omega Publications, 1998, front plate.

[3] I am indebted to Rabbi David Zaslow for this teaching which he got from his own teacher Rabbi Zalman Schacter-Shalomi who labeled the Testaments of the Bible the Elder and the Younger. It solves a problem where the phrase Old Testament is considered disrespectful and noting it as the Hebrew Bible is incomplete. I find this to be a very elegant teaching and a wonderful way of describing the two Testaments.

them using the oldest of principles; teachings based on nature and its cyclical wisdoms.

I was inspired both in my content and form by Neil Douglas-Klotz's work, especially his most excellent *Prayers of the Cosmos.* As Douglas-Klotz notes, by tradition, there are three ways that passages should be examined; intellectual, metaphorical and mystical. I love these designations. I use his basic concept but with slight differences. I use rational, symbolic and mystical.

In most chapters, I also follow Douglas-Klotz's lead of having three sections. The sections are as follows: First are one or more passages using the King James Version (KJV) for a traditional Biblical translation. This is followed by my own Mystic Pagan Version (MPV). In my own translations I strip out the gendered concepts of the divine unless crucial to understanding a passage. This is because Great Mystery, All Creation, all-divinity transcends duality.

I have a few translations from the New International Version (NIV) which highlight different aspects of the passages.

The second section contains my own commentary along with an explanation of how I arrived at each of the translations. When appropriate to the message, there will be a final section titled **Experiencing the Vibrational Essences**. This is the experiential section. Think of this as an adventure in spirituality. It is an opportunity to plug into the energetic aspect of the Hebrew, power syllables and the underlying meanings of the passages. For these sections, I invite you to make them your own. Experiment with the teachings, the chants, the body positions and see how they feel and operate in your own body. It's OK to mix and match the elements. Have fun and enjoy.

I use three lexicons as my primary sources:

1) Fabre d'Olivet, *The Hebraic Tongue Restored: And the True Meaning of the Hebrew Words Re-established and Proved by their Radical Analysis*, translated by Nayan Louise Redfield, Samuel Weiser, Inc. 1976 (first published

in 1921). d'Olivet looks at original root meanings of Hebrew words and often connects them to the roots of Arabic words as well.

2) Jeff A Benner, *Ancient Hebrew Lexicon of the Bible*, Virtualbookworm.com Publishing Inc, 2005. Benner looks at the ancient pictographs that are created by the root letters of a word. He uses these images to make a rebus as a way to look at their original meanings. In many cases, his meanings closely mirror those of d'Olivet.

3) *Strong's Concordance*. At times I will note the meaning of a word and include a "Strong's" citation indicated by an S and the number corresponding to the concordance. This is one of the primary compendiums of Hebrew Biblical words that list all the words, their roots and their meanings. Strong's meanings are agreed upon by most Biblical scholars and tend to be more traditional. I find them useful as a starting point. The reference number provides an opportunity for curious readers to look up the meanings of the words themselves. I recommend the site BibleHub.

Chapter 1 – The Magic of Chanting

Singing brings magic into the everyday world. We do not have to wait till we are in some ethereal place to hear the voices of angels – all we have to do is listen to our own singing and that of others who share our world with us. Singing is not an exalted, once in a lifetime miracle, but a joy to be shared whenever we like.
Carolyn Lee Boyd[4]

Chanting is sound medicine – medicine for everyone. There are so many beautiful chants and people who are able to sing these chants with remarkable voices. If you are one of these people, I adore listening to you with your soaring voices. It is a true gift and an uplifting spiritual experience.

Then there are people like me who struggle to find notes and can't hold a tune. Good news! We, too, can chant and in doing so experience and enjoy the power that it can bring. Whether we hold to one note, our voice wavers, or our tone changes and hurts our ears, the vibration of chanting is universal and does not rely on a beautiful singing voice. Chanting is cosmic medicine, whether witnessing, exploring sound, or singing.

---

[4] From the anthology, *Just as I Am: Hymns Affirming the Divine Female – A Girl God Hermnal*, Trista Hendren, editor, GirlGodBooks, 2021.

I have studied chanting with some teachers who have exquisite voices and I treasure those experiences. I adore listening. But it is not something I can replicate on my own. At first, I was worried that my own vocal clumsiness meant that avenue of chanting was closed for me. What I have learned, though, is that I can still have a personal practice that is fulfilling and even fun. If you have a calling and skill for music, enjoy that aspect, share it. I admire you. These chants can add to your repertoire. If you are like me and vocalizing is a challenge, use these chants to experiment and find your own voice.

Below, I note four different ways to approach chanting. All have merit. They can be combined. In each, I use *Hallelujah* (in its meaning of praise) as an example.

First: Song, performance, vibration. *Hallelujah* has been a particular focus of song-writing with beautiful results. The top results which come to my mind are Leonard Cohen and Handel. *Hallelujah* is a wonderful example of a performance chant and a choral piece.

Second: Seed syllables as the basis of chanting. Seed syllables are sounds that hold a vibrational power. In older cultures they tend to make up the names of deities. Some may be familiar to you: HA, AH, LA, AL, HU, EL, YA to name a few. Here again we can look at *Hallelujah* which means – praise Ya, praise God or praise divinity. The roots of the word are all seed syllables. Broken into component parts, they are – al-la-hu-yah (see chapter 11).

Third: Taking on the elements of what is being chanted. *Hallelujah* as a form of praising divinity, can be seen as a blessing. When we bless or praise something, we take on those same aspects. When we chant or sing *Hallelujah*, for example, we are taking on the qualities of both blessing and divinity.

Every single wisdom in the world has a particular chant,

a particular melody.
And when you chant that specific melody it will draw forth the
particular wisdom to which it is attached.
Rabbi Nachman of Breslav (1772-1810)[5]

Fourth: This approach is to feel the sense of oneness. It is using the vibrations to break down the barriers of myself and other, you and me, we and them, yin and yang, male and female.

This is the secret of the rooster's call:
At the time when God comes to the
Garden of Eden to visit those who have lived in balance, all the
trees in the Garden of Eden bring forth their fragrance
and break into song and praise.
At that very moment, here on Earth, the rooster is awakened by
the heavenly chanting and joins in,
singing its praise in seven calls.

Mirash Perek Shirah
Chapter of Song 4:1 (1500s)[6]

Chanting opens portals to feel/experience divine energies within ourselves. It creates channels between the worlds. This is why this book emphasizes how important it is to make the chanting our own. It is possible to chant using each of the levels, or several at the same time. This is true sacred play. Play away!

---

[5] In Gershon Winkler *Kabbalah 365,* Andrews McMeel Publishing, 2004, 106.
[6] Ibid, 305.

Chapter 2 – Creation

The Biblical story of creation occurs in the beginning of Genesis. In the translations that we are familiar with, the process involves separating out opposites.

As the Bible tells it, the progression of creation contains a separation into good (with its implied opposite bad), light and dark, heaven and earth, male and female. This story sets up a paradigm that maintains the concept of division. It's as if a wall came down and opposites became set and rigidly apart from each other.

This is a dualistic vision of the world. What if the teachings within the Bible were not dualistic, but taught of oneness, connection, and the flow of energy? A careful translation of the words indicates that the original teachings taught just this.

The key lies within the letters of the Biblically translated word "separation." The Hebrew word in Genesis is *bedel,* spelled with the letters *beyt* (B), *dal* (D), *lam* (L). In Hebrew, letters have meanings as well as sounds. *Beyt* means house. *Dal* or *dalet* means door, more specifically a tent door that swings in both directions to enter or exit the tent/house. *Lam* means staff, as in shepherd's staff, and is associated with authority, especially the authority of God.[7] Below are the letters of *bedel* (Hebrew is written from right to left):

---

[7] The staff is considered the origin of the magic wand and the royal scepter.

$$\text{ל} \qquad \text{ד} \qquad \text{ב}$$

lam   dal   beyt
L   D   B

If we put these letters together as a rebus, we get the following representation: a house (*beyt*) represents our earthly dwelling, and a staff (*lam*) represents divinity, the heavens. *Beyt* is an interesting letter that traditionally means house but in a broader sense can be interpreted as the Earth itself as our home. In between the two letters is a door (*dal*) as a tent flap. In this intrinsic meaning of separation, there is a passageway (door) between the earth (humanity, manifest) and the heavens (spirit, divinity).

$$\text{ל} \qquad\qquad \text{ד} \qquad\qquad \text{ב}$$

lam   *dalet*   *beyt*
divinity/creation   swinging door   earth/manifest

This, then, is not a separation shaped from impenetrable boundaries, but one of flowing movement. *Bedel*, decoded, describes the process of creation as **energy that flows through the tent door as it continues to move in both directions.**

Have you ever watched the dawn? Sunset? It is not light one minute and dark the next. The movement of the Earth creates both dawn and dusk as times when dark and light blend into one another. This creates a constant flow of motion, slipping from dark to light and back again in the course of a day. Other aspects that appear as opposites do the same.

Blending/harmony as the template of creation, and as part of our spiritual heritage, is a very different concept than we have come to know. This has profound implications for how we view our world. If separation is the paradigm of creation, then it becomes easier to see other people as separate from ourselves, creating a sense of "otherness." We see this in the endless ways we categorize and separate each other: by religion, nationality, race, gender. We are now experiencing a gender politics that sets up rigid roles of desired traits for "masculinity" and "femininity." And it does so in an angry, militant manner.

If gender is seen, as many scientists tell us, as a sliding scale of human experience then we, as a culture, have many options of behavior available to us. Such a belief guides us to accept variations and differences as part of the beautiful tapestry of the world. Indigenous populations have long had people in their community they name "two spirits." Two spirits not only remind us of what is possible, it allows people to live their authentic selves and bring back to their community the wisdom and practice of harmonizing apparent opposites.

The paradigm of blending/harmony also allows the space and understanding of mystical experiences as a normal and natural part of how the world works. This model guides us to appreciating how heavenly and otherworldly aspects are not separate from ourselves.

Another view of creation comes from the Gospel of John from the Younger Testament. He wrote, "in the beginning was the Word."

I expand that to say, "in the beginning was the word, the womb and the wisdom." This concept will be expanded throughout the book.

Spiritual leader, Matthew Fox has another interesting take; he said that "in the beginning was the energy."[8] This is a powerful concept that speaks to the vibration/movement of creation. This is what we will be working with.

---

[8] Verbal teaching from a class he taught called *The Path of Christ Consciousness*. (Unit 1, Class 4 7/8/25).

Chapter 3 – Mudra, Mantra, Mandala

Tete ka asom
Ancient things remain in the ears
The Asante Nation[9]

In eastern traditions, there is a three-pronged formula for manifestation. It is mudra, mantra and mandala. Mudra is a hand and/or body position. Mantra is a chant or vibrational sound. Mandala is an image for visualization. Alone, each of these elements has power but together they are even more commanding. Using these three in concert helps us to embody or co-create within ourselves the energy/power of the concepts.

The sections called **Experiencing the Vibrational Essences**, each contain a template of a mudra, mantra and mandala. This is an opportunity for each reader to plug into the energies revealed by this book. It is a practice that can serve many purposes.

It can be used as a spiritual model that deepens one's personal practice. It can be used as sacred play or just for pleasure. Other uses include specific manifestations. There are as many uses for this template as one's imagination can conceive.

Manifestation practices have the effect of co-creating our reality and our personal lives. When manifesting a quality or a specific request for our lives, intention matters.

-----

[9] Quote on Facebook page of The Asante Nation, Nov. 22, 2024.

There are several ways to focus on this. One is to work on qualities that you would like to increase in your own life. These can be potentials such as more forgiveness, releasing pain from trauma, more connection, more open-heartedness, energy flow, healing, abundance, creativity.

Another is to manifest a specific request such as a new car or a trip you'd like to take.

You can also head into this practice with no preconceived intent, just an openness and a question such as, "spirit, show me what I need to know."

In Hawaiian Huna, the spiritual/philosophical system from Aloha International, we also add a fourth element to the manifestation practice – an action. For example, if your intent is more forgiveness, your action can be to write a letter asking for forgiveness and/or you can write a letter granting forgiveness. You can write this letter to yourself or to another person. If it is to another person you can choose whether to send it or not. It might also help to read it out loud either to another person or even to a tree. When complete, you can burn it, hold it, bury it. These are powerful techniques to let go of pain surrounding a wounding in your spirit.

If you are looking to increase your creativity you can keep crayons nearby or beads or craft paper. If your intent is for a new car, you can begin a jar for loose change to gather financial resources, or you might buy a toy car to put in a prominent location. This becomes a message to your inner self that holds the focus of your intent. If your intent is to let spirit guide you, then smudge your room or even use your breath as an honoring.

Personal story: *There was a time when I wanted to travel to Greece. Money was tight and our family situation wasn't conducive. I followed these practices and in a final action put a Greek coin on my desk. I used that coin as spirit magnet to draw my energies towards Greece. It worked. I not only managed to manifest that trip, but some family members joined me.*

When playing with the **Experiencing the Vibrational Essences** section, be sure to listen to your own heart, your own voice and your own body. I make suggestions for mudras for the hands and/or full body. This is never meant to be painful. For example, if the mudra of holding arms up becomes too much, feel free to fold them onto your torso, at the heart area, the navel area, or the third eye. These can all be done standing, sitting or even lying down.

If you want to shout a mantra, go for it. If you want to hum instead, that works as well. Be as quiet as a buzzing bee. Be as loud as a roaring lion. You can put on a recording and listen to chanting or singing. Follow your heart, listen to your inner guidance.

This work is based on teachings of our ancestors that were preserved and gifted to us, their descendants. This practice carries the marrow, the spirit of their deep-rooted experiences. For some of the mudras, I have included photos of ancient artifacts that illustrate not only poses, but also the treasure of spirit work left behind by our ancestors. This is the gift that has reached out to us from the mists of time.

Chapter 4 – Biblical Names of Divinity
El, YHVH, Shaddai

You who revere the
Creator of the boundless universe,
Call him Jehova or God,
Call him Fu, or Brahma.
Hark! Hark to the words
Of the Almighty's trumpet call!
Ringing out through earth, moon, sun,
Its sound is everlasting.

Written for
Mozart Cantata K. 619[10]

The original names used for divinity in the Bible cannot be recognized in English versions because they are translated away from their original Hebrew. In translation, the two most frequently used divine names are God and LORD. God is the frequent

---

[10] Jan Assman, *Moses the Egyptian,* Harvard University Press, 1997; 136. The following is Assman's footnote; 249. "The text is by Franz Hermann Ziegenhagen (1733-1806), a pietist, Spinozist, Freemason, and pedagogue who devised a new program of adult education based on the study of nature and who commissioned the cantata from Mozart for the inauguration ceremony of his institute in the summer of 1791." Translation is by Solomon.

translation for many Hebrew terms, El or Elohim the most common. El is used 238 times in the Bible and Elohim, over 2,500 times.

El or Elohim is the Great God from Genesis 1 who set in motion All-Creation. But El as deity was even older. To the Canaanites, in pre-Biblical history, El was known as the "great bull God."

The "im" in Elohim is a plural suffix. In Hebrew, plural suffixes have several meanings. As in English, plurals refer to quantity meaning more than one; one tree, two trees. In Hebrew, plural can also mean one which is the most glorious, most sublime of all. For example, in this manner "one trees" can mean that the single tree referenced is grander, bigger and more wonderful than all others. In this system, Elohim can be one divinity in all the grandeur of creation, or it can be plural, more than one divinity. Or it can be both. Spiritual writing tends to be multi-layered. Elohim as a concept can be the Great God El as well as his "wife," the Great Bull Goddess, sometimes known as Isis who wore bull horns as one of her headdresses.

Elohim, in its original meanings, elevates the Great Sacred Mystery of Creation out of duality. Elohim is transcendent of gender.

The ancient Semitic meaning of El is mighty or strength. I translate El as All-Potential because of its transcendence and connection with fertility. El is both God and Goddess. My original translation was All-Potential Powers but now I have removed the "powers" to recognize that All-Potential encompasses many layers of meanings. It does not only refer to "power" but also to creative functioning, nurturing life, the magic of creation. In other words, All-Potential.

Whenever you see the term LORD in the Bible, the Hebrew behind it is always the same. They are four sacred letters or vowels called the Tetragrammaton (tetra meaning four). The Hebrew letters are *yud-hey-vav-hey*. These are transliterated into English (the Latin alphabet) as YHVH. Scholars have forever argued about its meaning and pronunciation. Vowel sounds used in an utterance or a word have powerful vibratory essences which is why many of the ancient names for divinity are made up from these vibrations. Vowels in a word are the vibratory batteries; four vowels together become a confluence of energies. Although I, too, do not know how or if these were pronounced, I do have some ideas based on the resonances they transmit.

When I began this work, I wanted to have one consistent translation for YHVH. But that was narrow thinking on my part. Its meaning is so multi-layered and filled with so much mystery that I found different interpretations were appropriate in different passages and circumstances.

***

Story Interlude

This is a story that can be used as a meditation on the power of vibration along with the energy of the holy names.

I have set my rainbow in the clouds,
and it will be the sign of the covenant between me and the earth.
Genesis 9:13 NIV

When time and timelessness were yet one, a wisdom bringer traveled amongst the stars. It could have been Satet, the archer with the heart of a warrior or it could have been Moses or his sister Miriam, or Abraham, Sarah, Hagar or any number of other prophets who once came to remind us that the divine is present among us at all times.

The wisdom bringer began a quest to collect all the treasures of Creation in an earthenware jar. The first step was to form a foundational brew from the ingredient of sacred silence. The wisdom bringer continued this mission until the jar was almost filled to the brim with the light and fire of the stars, the dripping dews of the heavens, and the names of all the creation deities. Added to these were loud noises, roars, thunders, the cries of newborn babies, the moans of lovers, the ackkkk's of the eagle, and the "I am's."

The earthenware jar, turned cauldron, was set upon a large fire and boiled until distilled down to one precious drop of liquid.

From this cauldron, our wisdom-bringer poured that single drop into the Nile or it could have been the Ganges or the Tigris or the Yangtze or the Amazon.

This caused the waters to flood and bring all nourishment to manifestation upon the Earth. As that precious drop arched downwards to its destination, it appeared in the heavens as a rainbow. A promise of heaven's bounty for time upon time.

***

Below are the four translations I use in this book and a short discussion of why.

YaaaHaaaVaaaHaaa echoes the vibrational undulations of the sacred sounds. This translation adds the vowel sound "aaah," which is also a universal breath sound, to each of the four sacred letters. It gives each reader an opportunity to take a deep breath and experience the vibrational resonances of the syllables in our bodies. Chanting these sounds is a powerful way to connect with divine energies. In fact, chanting is en-chant-ment. It is magical and this is your invitation to step into the magic. The idea for this translation comes from a meditation called the *tseruf*[11] from the 12th century mystic and kabbalist Abraham Abulafia. More information about the complete chant can be found in Appendix 1. This name as chant is featured in Chapter 12.

---

[11] *Tseruf* means transformation.

Mother/Father Creator as translation transcends duality and gender just as Elohim does. This is explicit in the letters. H is often transliterated from the Hebrew letter *hey* because they have a similar sound quality. But this is a transliteration meaning there is no single one to one correlation. Here is another option. *Hey* is the 5th letter of the Hebrew *aleph-beit*. The 5th letter of the English alphabet is E which also has a similar sound quality. If we swap out the H for an E, we get YEVE.

Notice Eve, the Great Goddess from the Garden of Eden, sitting right there in the middle of this most sacred name of divinity. Y or Yud is considered shorthand for the supernal male energy and Eve is the supernal female energy. The two together become Mother/Father Creator.

Great Mystery represents creation and vibrant life. What happens before we come to earth and what happens after are great mysteries. Why are we here? A great mystery. Divinity is the source and manifestation of mystery. We are formed from mystery and carry it within us as we experience the many wonders of embodied life on our earth-walk.

Vibration.Being is in juxtaposition to human.being. *Being* is the essence of life, the *beingness* of life is existence or in Neil Douglas-Klotz's brilliant assessment, "livingness, life energy coming into being."[12] *Beingness* transcends mundane earth-based existence. It is a mystical, mysterious state. *Vibration* is used to indicate how sound – music, chant, thunder, roaring – are all aspects of the cacophony that set creation in motion. *Vibration.Being*[13] is the divine representation of that process. I use

---

[12] Neil Douglas-Klotz, *Revelations of the Aramaic Jesus, The Hidden Teachings on Life & Death*, prologue.
[13] When I use the dot between words that is a nod to the work of Jeff Benner who uses the concept to connect words that are not typically linked but do have a connection.

this term *Vibration.Being* in parallel to *human.being* or more broadly, *humanity.being*.

Humanity in shamanic circles doesn't just refer to human life but to all life. The term refers to shells, pavement, rocks, metals, stars, all of creation.

> *So God created man in his own <u>image</u>,*
> *in the <u>image</u> of God created he him;*
> Genesis 1:27

The word for image is *tselem*. *Tselem* is another multi-layered word that means more than just image, it is an aspect of, a reflection that contains the original. I will often use reflection even though this, too, is an imperfect translation. Here is my longer definition: *Tselem* encompasses a full-bodied, essential (as in essence) aspect filled with powerful divinely inspired vibration, directly from the source. For more on this word see Appendix 2.

I use this translation (along with YaaaHaaaVaaaHaaa) to come as close as I can to the vibrational essence of this holy name. English doesn't have the vibrational quality to replicate it perfectly. Human.being, the term we name ourselves, is the image, the reflection of Vibration.Being. Together, they parallel the relationship of the manifest to the divine. Or the earth to the heavens.

To add to the multi-layered aspect and as noted above, the word for "being" isn't quite right either. "Being" by itself is a static word. The Hebrew word is *hayah* which is dynamic, alive, holding within it the concept of becoming, transitioning, emerging or unfolding. Its root is related to the Hebrew name of Eve. *Hayah* speaks to a process not a static event. Perhaps a more accurate translation would be:

> *Roaring vibration.dynamic unfolding with*
> *emergent.livingness.dynamism*

A mouthful to be sure!

Seed.being represents the beingness or the roaring, vibrational dynamism of seeds along with their potential to hold life and transport it to all corners of the Earth.

Shaddai

The phrase *El Shaddai* or *Shaddai* appears 48 times in the Bible, first appearing when Mother/Father Creator speaks to Abraham in Genesis 17:1.

In English, *El Shaddai* is usually translated as "God Almighty" with *Shaddai* as "Almighty." Sometimes they are translated as "God, the One of the Mountain."[14] Both are almost always referred to in scholarly discussions with the pronoun "he." This is curious since the root of *Shaddai* is *shad* meaning breasts or teats.

Shaddai is a divinity with breasts and so unlikely to be male.

---

[14] *The Jewish Study Bible*, 37.

Chapter 5 – The Personal Name of Divinity

O Thou, the Breathing Life of all, Creator
of the shimmering sound that touches us.
Neil Douglas-Klotz[15]

<u>Exodus 3:13-15</u>

3:13: And Moses said unto God, Behold, *when* I come unto the children of Israel, and shall say unto them, The God of your fathers hath sent me unto you; and they shall say to me, What *is* his name? what shall I say unto them?

3:14: And God said unto Moses, I AM THAT I AM: and he said, Thus shalt thou say unto the children of Israel, I AM hath sent me unto you.

3:15: And God said moreover unto Moses, Thus shalt thou say unto the children of Israel, The LORD God of your fathers, the God of Abraham, the God of Isaac, and the God of Jacob, hath sent me

---

[15] Neil Douglas-Klotz, *The Prayers of the Cosmos*, his original translation of "Our father who art in heaven."

unto you: this *is* my name for ever, and this *is* my memorial unto all generations. This shall be My name forever.
KJV

3:13: Moses said to Elohim, When I come to the Israelites, and say to them, All-Potential of your ancestors has sent me to you; and they ask me, What is All-Potential's name? What shall I say to them?"

3:14: And All-Potential said to Moses, LIFE UNFOLDING[16] blessed LIFE UNFOLDING. Thus shall you say to the Israelites, EHYEH sent me to you.

3:15: And All-Potential said further to Moses, Thus shall you speak to the Israelites, Mother/Father Creator of All-Potential, divinity of your ancestors, Abraham and Sarah, Isaac and Rachel, Jacob and Rebekah, has sent me to you: this shall be how I am known throughout all-time. This is my essence for now and throughout all-beingness.
MPV

---

[16] I am indebted to Rabbi Jonathan Kligler of the Woodstock Jewish Congregation for this translation of *ehyeh*.

COMMENTARY

The core of this passage lies in Exodus 3:14 where Moses has asked for the personal name of divinity and is answered. The traditional translation is I AM THAT I AM. In phonetic Hebrew it is *ehyeh-asher-ehyeh.*

In this passage we run into the same motifs with "beingness" that we encountered with Vibration.Being. It is "beingness" or "becomingness" as a process.

Exodus 3:14 is a surprisingly complex and multi-layered declaration. As with YHVH, in English we don't have adequate words to translate it with the full constellation of its meanings. The I AM or *ehyeh* has the same root as *hayah (hey yud hey). Hayah* is a word that means "life" or "to be" which is how the translation commonly becomes I AM. This is shorthand for a more complex and beautiful declaration. *Hayah* is related to all 3 tenses of time; past, present and future. It means all at the same time: I was, I am, I will be. This is existence that is not tethered to linear time as we here on Earth experience it. In its fullness, divinity's name is a variant of "beingness."[17]

I have struggled with this translation. I settled on the one above using Rabbi Kligler's LIFE UNFOLDING for *ehyeh* and then using the Hebrew itself for the shorthand name.

The small word in the center translated to THAT is also more complicated and layered than at first glance. It is *asher* using the root letters *shin-resh* or the sounds *sh-r.* It is the root of the name of the Goddess Ashera and the matriarch Sarah. The term asher(ot) or asher(im) is used in the Bible as a tree or trees (groves). Although rarely translated it is commonly understood to represent Ashera the Goddess. This same word root is also used to mean sing, blessing and umbilical cord. I haven't uncovered one translation that encompasses all, so I am presenting a playful look at possibilities which seen all together as one give us a sense of the

---

[17] Kenneth Hanson, *Kabbalah: The Untold Story of the Mystic Tradition,* Council Oak, 2004, 25.

meanings. I am also including a list of words I considered for the translation of *ehyeh*[18]:

<u>Word List for *ehyeh*</u>:

>Creative-ing
>Creation-ing
>Existence-ing
>Life-ing
>Eve-isness
>Unfolding
>Flowering

Fun with **Exodus 3:14**

I am that I am.
I am blessed, I am
I AM Ashera, I AM

Unfolding, blessed, unfolding
Becomingness, fecundity, becomingness

I am motion-filled song, I move
I am the umbilicus through which I flow, I flow
I vibrate birthing, I vibrate

I AM Ashera, EVE
EVE, Ashera, EVE

---

[18] This is all inspired by the translations from Neil Douglas Klotz, Kenneth Hanson and Rabbi Kliger as well as works by David Elkington.

EXPERIENCING THE VIBRATIONAL ESSENCES

Mantra

Ehyeh-asher-ehyeh

The syllables drawn out, sound like this: *Ayyy-yehhh, ash-air, ayyy-yehhh*

Both of these phrases are composed of power syllables or sounds that resonate through our bodies and connect us to these dynamic energies. When chanting these syllables, take time to feel the sounds as they move across your tongue. Pay attention to the energy of the sounds as they move through your body. Feel free to linger on a particular sound if you find one that harmonizes for you. Enjoy the resonances of the syllables.

Emphasize each sound. Slur them together. Sing them! Chant them. Make the tones buzz like a honeybee! Have fun! Make it your own. As I wrote previously, this is sacred play.

Chanting or saying out loud "I AM" in English can also have strong overtones and vibrations.

Mandala

A wonderful image to use for this meditation is a tree. Try using different trees. Perhaps a favorite one. One with leaves. One whose branches are bare. Oak, cedar, juniper, beech, maple. Large trunks and smaller ones. I suggest trees for this particular mantra because of the connection to Ashera and Her tree groves. You can also use an actual tree if that works for you.

Mudra

Announce your presence, place your hands in the air, palms facing outwards. Feel the energy move across your palms. Feel your rootedness in the ground. Below are two artifacts from the ancients who also used this pose. I use them to illustrate that in many cultures and throughout time, these postures have been recognized for their ability to hold power.

The purpose of the mudra is to feel the energetic potentials they hold. It is not to do an iron-man type of session. You can move so the pose does not become uncomfortable. For example, if you are sitting brace your elbows on the armrests. If you are standing brace them on furniture. After you have gathered the energy essence of the pose, you can also lower your hands to one of your chakras such as placing them over your heart or your belly. Swaying, nodding, dancing works too.

Ishtar vase, Louvre. The goddess Isthar, winged and wearing a version of the horned cap of divinity, 2nd millennium BCE. photo by Marie-Lan Nguyen, Wikimedia commons, public domain.

Goddess with upraised arms.
Terracotta, Kania, Gortys, 1300-
1200 BCE. Archaeological
museum of Heraklion, photo by
Zde, Wikimedia commons.

Chapter 6 – Joyful Noise
Psalm 98:4-5, Numbers 21:17, and Psalm 105:2-3

All lives, all dances, and all is loud.[19]

<u>Psalm 98:4-5</u>

Make a joyful noise unto the LORD, all the earth: make a loud noise, and rejoice, and sing praise.
Sing unto the LORD with the harp; with the harp, and the voice of a psalm.
KJV

Make a joyful noise unto all the Great Mystery of creation, to all the Earth
Burst forth loudly with shouts of joy and songs of praise, shout, sing, rejoice, play instruments, be loud.
MPV

---

[19] Rachel Pollack wrote about this concept in her *Shining Tribe Tarot* book regarding the Seven of Birds. The quote comes from Bruce Chatwin's *The Songlines*.

<u>**Numbers 21:17**</u>

Then Israel sang this song, Spring up, O well; sing ye unto it:
KJV

Then the people sang this song, Arise O wellspring of the Earth,
re-sound the tremble of the verses.
MPV

<u>**Psalm 105:2-3**</u>

Sing unto him, sing psalms unto him: talk ye of all his wondrous
works.
Glory ye in his holy name: let the heart of them rejoice that seek
the LORD.
KJV

Sing, vibrate, pluck strings, bang drums
Connect with erotic, creative, sacred powers.
For the vibrations of Great Mystery resound in the hearts of those
who quest.
MPV

COMMENTARY

In the beginning was the Word, and the Word was with God,
and the Word was God.
John 1:1

In this chapter, I begin the process of translating different verses and putting them into groups. In this grouping the verses extol music, noise and their roles in creation. They all discuss the vibration, movement, and energetic aspects of sound and syllable that connect us to mystery, life and growth.

This concept reflects and embraces the foundational essence of "beingness" or as we have seen it in Hebrew *ehyeh* and its root-mate *hayah*.

This is embodied spirituality in its most basic form. It uses the instrument of our bodies to connect with the energies of our world and beyond. In using our voices, and plugging into sound, this becomes a personal embodied experience. This practice becomes an opportunity to feel and experience the myriad gifts this world and creation have to offer.

EXPERIENCING THE VIBRATIONAL ESSENCES

Mantra

The Hebrew song from Numbers 21:17 is *Spring up, O well; sing ye unto it* in the KJV's traditional translation. My MPV translation is *Arise O wellspring of The Earth, re-sound the tremble of the verses*. The song in Hebrew is filled with power syllables. Here are its phonetic sounds:

Ay-lee beh-air ay-new-lah

Or stretching the syllables out:

Ayyy-leeeee beeeeehh-ayyyyer aiiiii-new-lahhhhh

For this mantra, practice the syllables to feel them in your body. Pay attention to how the syllables set up energy waves. Different sounds will resonate in different manners, even at different times of the day or at different seasons. For everyone this will be individual.

Another way to use this chant is to break out the syllables. You can choose the syllable set that most speaks to you.

1) *ayyy-leeeee*
2) *beeeeehh-ayyyyer*
3) *aiiiii-new-lahhhhh*

Mandala

Picture the wind whistling through the leaves of the trees, the breath as it moves through a conch shell or a ram's horn, the singing of birds, a rainbow. See what best vibrates with you. Feel free to experiment with these or with alternate images of your own.

Mudra

This posture is similar to the one in Chapter 5. It adds the element of bird imagery and feeling. The emphasis is on being uplifted as if the arms are wings that are lifting to the sky. Hands are facing upward and inward. The same notes from Chapter 4's mudra hold true here. You do not need to experience discomfort from the pose.

Terracotta Mycenaean bird goddess figurines Tiryns NAM Nafplio Greece 1400-1100 BCE, photo by Mary Harrsch, Wikimedia Commons.

Standing female figurine of the "goddess with uplifted arms" type. Cypriot, Statuette of a votary c. 600-480 BCE. Wikimedia Commons, donated as part of a project by the Metropolitan Museum of Art.

Chapter 7 – The Divine As Music
Exodus 15:2, Isaiah 6:3, and Isaiah 44:23

*The singing of words reveals their true meanings directly to the
soul through bodily vibration.*
Hildegard of Bingen[20]

Exodus 15:2

The LORD *is* my strength and song, and he is become my
salvation: he *is* my God, and I will prepare him an habitation; my
father's God, and I will exalt him.
KJV

YaaaHaaaVaaaHaaa is my radiance and song,
unveiling pathways of reclamation
rooted in the heart of our ancestors,
resplendent in beauty.
MPV

---

[20] From *Physica*, translated by Priscilla Throop. Quoted in David Elkington's
book *The Ancient Language of Sacred Sound.*

<u>**Isaiah 6:3**</u>

And one cried unto another, and said, Holy, holy, holy, *is* the LORD of hosts: the whole earth *is* full of his glory.
KJV
And each called to each and said Holy holy, holy is Great Mystery: our earth filled with the glory of all that is divine.
MPV

<u>**Isaiah 44:23**</u>

Sing, O ye heavens; for the LORD hath done *it*: shout, ye lower parts of the earth: break forth into singing, ye mountains, O forest, and every tree therein
KJV

Sing praises for Great Mystery's treasure,
honor the depths of the earth with the pulse of your voice.
Let your singing resound to embrace mountains, forests and trees.
MPV

COMMENTARY

As discussed in the previous section, the process of sound vibration works in our bodies to create an embodied spirituality that is particularly powerful. Our vocal cords are key. We need to breathe in air and let it cross our vocal cords to chant and to sing. In fact, to talk and express ourselves at all.

As previously noted, sacred languages such as Hebrew tend to be made up of power syllables that, when verbalized, resonate in our bodies. The vibrational aspects of such language give us the ability to gain experiential embodied knowledge.

In Isaiah 6:3 the phrase *holy, holy, holy* is the word *qadosh* (Strong's 6918) repeated 3 times. It comes from the same root as a word from Genesis 38:21 *qedeshah* (Strong's 6948). *Qedeshah* is translated as harlot, temple prostitute, shrine prostitute, among others. In other words, *Qadosh* as holy and *qedeshah* as harlot have the same root.

Historians trace the connection of *qedeshah* with sexual acts to an interpretation by the historian Herodotus in the 5th century BCE. It is a connection that has stuck and can be seen in the well-known concept of temple prostitutes. Feminists feel this is a misogynistic read because it implies that women can only be powerful through the agency of sex. I believe this whole brouhaha misses the point.

I believe *qedeshah* describes a fundamental energy. I think of the essay by Audre Lorde titled "The Uses of the Erotic" with the subtitle, "The Power of the Erotic." Lorde points out that though the erotic can be related to the sexual act in particular, it is far larger and grander at its core. It encompasses the passionate energy of an artist, a soul in the act of creativity, a person fully in their bodies and flowing with power. As Lorde writes, "The erotic is the nurturer or nursemaid of all our deepest knowledge."

Cynthia Bourgeault also makes this point when she writes, "Without the quicksilver of eros nothing transforms."[21] This, to me, is *qedeshah* and it is holy.

Qadosh is a fundamental energy that underlies life and creation. This is sacred and it is experienced through our human bodies. This all comes together to make the word root *qadash* a powerful, vibratory energy. Excellent for a chant.

---

[21] Cynthis Bourgeault, *The Meaning of Mary Magdalene*, (Shambala, 20120), 94.

EXPERIENCING THE VIBRATIONAL ESSENCES

Mantra

Holy, holy, holy from Isaiah 6:3 is *quadosh, quadosh, quadosh* in Hebrew.

Mandala

Because *quadosh* is a power word. Think of an image that holds power for you. Clouds opening to a bright sky over a mountaintop, a rainbow, a waterfall. Someone you love.

Mudra

The primary focus for this mudra involves the head. It is to place our head in an upward position with eyes facing upward and the neck slightly extended. Necks can be tricky so it is most important to find a comfortable position. Mouth is slightly open. The hands and rest of the body can be placed in positions that work for you so feel free to experiment. Following is one possibility that has been left to us by our ancestors.

Standing figure, Mexico, Olmec, 900 BCE, serpentine. De Young Museum, photo by Daderot, Wikimedia commons.

Chapter 8 – Carrying Seeds
Genesis 2:10 and Psalm 36:8

Genesis 2:10

And a river went out of Eden to water the garden; and from thence it was parted, and became into four heads.
KJV

Life giving waters cascaded out from Eden to nourish and scatter seed.beings to become the beginning.
MPV

Psalm 36:8

They shall be abundantly satisfied with the fatness of thy house; and thou shalt make them drink of the river of thy pleasures.
 KJV

Drink with abundance of the freely flowing waters, for these waters carry the treasure seeds of life's inheritance.
MPV

COMMENTARY

Psalm 36:8 not only echoes Genesis 2:10, it enhances the narrative of the life-giving aspects of the seeds. Let's take a closer look at the first line of Genesis 2:10 highlighting the two different translations

And a river went out of Eden to water the garden (KJV)

Life giving waters cascaded out from Eden to nourish (MPV)

The watering of the garden is described after the river has left Eden, so it is watering a garden someplace else. The assumption is that this water flowing out of Eden is nourishing gardens at Earth locations. The Hebrew word for garden is *gan*. One translation of *gan* is "a gathering of seeds."[22] When the waters left Eden, they were carrying the seeds that had been gathered, possibly created, there.

The word for river in KJV and life-giving waters in MPV is *nahar* (Strong's 5104). One of the meanings of *nahar* is "the life-giving water that washes over soil."[23] Its root also gives rise to the Hebrew word *nhara* (Strong's 5094)[24] which means enlightenment or wisdom. These are special waters indeed to be carrying wisdom along with the fertile seeds.

And now to look at the second line of Genesis 2:10 from the two perspectives.

and from thence it was parted, and became into four heads.
(KJV)

and scatter seed.beings to become the beginning. (MPV)

---

[22] Benner, 83.
[23] Benner, 190.
[24] Ibid.

The word that KJV translates to "parted," and I translate to "scatter," is the Hebrew word *parad* (Strong's 6504). This is root-related to a word for seed which Benner describes: "As separated from the parent plant and scattered in the field."[25] The point is that seeds are all over this passage which describes the process of creation itself as it manifests on Earth.

The word for [four] "heads" (Strong's 7218) is closely related to the first word of the Bible in Genesis 1:1 *bereshyt* (Strong's 7225). This is traditionally translated as "in the beginning." Its more literal meaning is "in the summit."[26]

I love the juxtaposition of the two beginnings in Genesis 1:1 and Genesis 2:10. The start of Genesis is the beginning of all creation. Genesis 2:10 describes the beginning of the scattering of seeds which can symbolically be recognized as life rooting into the Earth. It is easy to recognize how water that gives life is carrying seeds within it.

The word *eden* (Strong's 5730) is a noun that means pleasure or delight.

---

[25] Benner, 419. *Perudah* (Strong's 6507) the seed that is separated from the kernel. Can also mean grain.

[26] I considered using "four directions" in this translation as the lays out of the map of time/space into a manifestation that allows for creation here on Earth. The four directions set up this paradigm.

EXPERIENCING THE VIBRATIONAL ESSENCES

Mantra

The phonetic pronunciation of Psalm 36:8 is:

ay-den-nika tasha-queeem

With the syllables drawn out:

aiiiiii-den-neeee-kaaaa tashaaaaa-kweeeeeem

In some of the Hebrew word-sounds, I have recommended breaking out the syllables. While it will work with this one, using the full syllabication has a strong resonance which flows in a special way. Experiment with using different cadences; slow and drawn out, quick and energetic, melodic and flowing.

Mandala

The flowing of water which carries seeds. River, waterfall, tidal waves, etc . . .

Mudra

Experiment with hand positions to feel which ones increase the feeling of flow. Some suggestions: palms up, hands on heart, hands on hara which is just below the belly button.

Extra Ideas

Have the words flow as water does. Allow the vibrations of these words to fill your body. Allow them to flow around you. Picture the seeds that are being planted in you, outside of you, in your environs. What are those seeds?

Even if you don't know what the seeds are, imagine what they look like, how the roots will grow, the first shoots, ways that you can nurture them. Are the seeds small or large? Are they mottled or are they one color? Red? Brown? Green? Yellow? The more detailed you can be, the more real they will feel.

Chapter 9 – Heart Wisdom
Proverbs 4:23 and Ecclesiastes 3:11

<u>Proverbs 4:23</u>

Keep thy heart with all diligence;
for out of it *are* the issues of life.
KJV

Above all else, guard your heart,
for everything you do flows from it.
NIV

Shepherd your heart with all that nourishes
for it is the wellspring of your life.
MPV

<u>Ecclesiastes 3:11</u>

He hath made every *thing* beautiful in his time:
also he hath set the world in their heart,

so that no man can find out the work that God maketh from the
beginning to the end.
KJV

As creation continues to flow,
everything is wondrous in its season,
infused with wisdom lodged in blossoming hearts
shrouded by divine mystery interwoven throughout
manifest time.
MPV

COMMENTARY

These passages are about the wisdom that we all carry in our hearts. I love the New International Version of Proverbs 4:23, but I do have a hesitation. The translation says "guard your heart" which is a turn of the phrase having several meanings.

When someone is "en garde" or in a guarded position, that indicates a stress posture. When we guard something, it introduces a sense of tension. Injecting any stress into the meditative aspect of this proverb inhibits the very flow of energy that is being discussed.

Ecclesiastes 3:11 is a beautiful passage with mystical aspects. It speaks about the cycle of the seasons and the juxtaposition of divine or heavenly time which cannot be measured as opposed to earthly time which is linear and is measured from the beginning to the end. As *humanity.beings* we have roots in both.

EXPERIENCING THE VIBRATIONAL ESSENCES

Mantra

The phonetic pronunciation of "your heart" in Proverbs 4:23 is lib-be-ka (Stong's 3820). For this chant I have added the word for blessing:

lib-be-ka br-ka

The syllables drawn out:

leeee-beh-kaahhh brrrrr-kaaahhhhh

The "brrrr" sound is guttural so that you feel it in your chest. The word *br-ka* means blessing in a way of giving honor to another or a gifting.

Mandala

Focus on the concept of a flower heart. Flowers are diverse, bring us beauty, sensuous aromas, and open to the world in vulnerability and grace. As you feel the movement of your heart, imagine a flower overlaying it. Let the flower gently open.

Mudra

Rub your palms together to heat your hands and then place them over your heart.

Chapter 10 – Trees and Seeds

Genesis 1:11, Genesis 2:8 and Genesis 3:8

<u>Genesis 1:11</u>

And God said, Let the earth bring forth grass,
the herb yielding seed, and the fruit tree yielding fruit
after his kind, whose seed is in itself, upon the earth:
and it was so.
KJV

And All-Potential vibrated, calling for earth's energy
to awaken seeds in diversity and in service of life enduring
that fruits from seeds bear seeds:
and all exists so
MPV

<u>Genesis 2:8</u>

And from the ground the LORD God caused to grow every tree
that was pleasing to the sight and good for food,
with the tree of life in the middle of the garden,

and the tree of knowledge of good and bad.
KJV

Vibration.Being of All-Potential ignited and awakened life
propelling beauty and the sweetness of fruits.
The grand Tree of Eve at the core of the garden
and the tree of growing into the duality of linear time.
MPV

Genesis 3:6

And when the woman saw that the tree was good for food,
and that it was pleasant to the eyes,
and a tree to be desired to make one wise,
she took of the fruit thereof, and did eat,
and gave also unto her husband with her; and he did eat.
KJV

When the womyn saw the tree, she recognized Herself
She remembered beauty and wisdom
She took its seeds within her in knowing wholeness
She gifted its seeds to her partner in loving wholeness.
MPV

COMMENTARY

We, as *humanity.beings,* have a deep connection to trees. So much so that it is reflected in our language. Even today, we speak about our own ancestors as "the roots" of our "family tree" of which there are many "branches." Our descendants are "offshoots." Our children are the "fruit" of our loins.

Anthropologist and religious scholar Mircea Eliade writes extensively about the associations of trees and their ancestral connection to humans. He calls them both mystical and mythical.[27] His examples include the Miao groups of Southern China and Southeast Asia who "worship the bamboo as their ancestor." He also notes Australian tribes who view the mimosa as their progenitor. And there is a tribe from Madagascar called Antaivandrika which means "people of the tree." They consider themselves descended from the banana tree.

The Hebrew language provides further evidence of our relationship to trees. In Hebrew the word for tree is *ets*. If you add the universal breath syllable, *ah* (or *ha*) you get *ets-ah* which means spine (or sacrum). *Ets-eem*[28] in Hebrew means bones. We all carry our own trees of life within our human bodies. Our bones are likened to the bones of trees. Our spines are our personal trees of life. In this way they are deeply connected to the trunk/spines of the trees.

Eve is *chavah* or *hawwah* depending on the transliteration. In Hebrew, the "Tree of Life" is the tree of *ha-hay-yim* or Her name in plural.

The Tree of Life, literally translated, means the Tree of Eve (transcendent of gender) in its grandest, most powerful aspect. The

---

[27] Mircea Eliade, *Patterns of Comparative Religion*, translated by Rosemary Sheed, University of Nebraska Press, 1996, 300-301.

[28] Or *ets-eem*, a plural form of the word tree.

51

Hebrew *ha-hay-yim*[29] is life in plural, LIFE/EVE writ large in the fullness of all mystery.

Seeds are one of the primary ways that life is dispersed here on Earth. Adam and Eve, so the story goes, ate from the fruit of the tree. As scientist Thor Hanson writes, "Fruit, in all its magnificent variety, exists for no other reason than to serve the seeds." In fact, Hanson continues, Adam and Eve were the original Biblical agents of dispersal. After eating the seed-rich fruit, they were expelled from the garden carrying their seeds with them inside their bodies. He continues, "With that one tempting fruit, it [the tree with its abundance of seeds] went from a garden-bound existence to the promise of mass dispersal with humanity across the face of the earth."[30]

---

[29] The "w" and "y" are interchangeable. The "*eem*" or "*yim*" sound at the end is the plural suffix.

[30] Thor Hanson, *The Triumph of Seeds*, Basic Books, 2015, 182-184.

EXPERIENCING THE VIBRATIONAL ESSENCES

Mantra

Ets, Ets-ah, ets-eem,
Etzzzzzz, etz-ahhhhhhhhhh, etz-eeeeeem

Mudra and Mandala

Stand with your heart directly against a tree. If possible and practical, remove as many clothing barriers as you can between the tree and your heart. Other positions to experiment with are the forehead (third eye) against the tree or standing with your back (spine) against the tree. Close your eyes and feel the energy, the rhythms. Try this in different places. See if the feelings and the rhythms change and in what way.

Practice reaching for the sap moving in the tree just as our blood moves within our body.

If you don't have immediate access to be close to a tree, you can either use a house plant, a piece of wood and if neither of those is available, your imagination will work too.

.

Thank, bless, honor and love the experience, thank, bless, honor and love the trees.

Chapter 11 – Celebration of Trees
Deut 20:19, Psalm 1:3 and Proverbs 3:18

<u>Deut 20:19</u>

…thou shalt not cut them down (for the tree of the field *is* man's *life*) . . .
KJV

. . .thou shalt cherish them (for the trees of the field are the brother/sister journeyers of our lives) . . .
MPV

<u>Psalm 1:3</u>

And he shall be like a tree planted by the rivers of water,
that bringeth forth his fruit in his season;
his leaf also shall not wither; and whatsoever he doeth shall prosper.
KJV

And we shall be likened to trees, planted by the flowing rivers
Bringing forth fruits in the fullness of time
So that our seeds may flourish.
MPV

<u>**Proverbs 3:18**</u>

She *is* a tree of life to them that lay hold upon her: and happy *is every one* that retaineth her.
KJV

She is a tree of life to those who acclaim Her, and blessed are all who embrace Her.
MPV

COMMENTARY

In the previous section we established our personal connections to trees. This section takes the next step of celebrating and honoring trees as an element of our relationship to them. Trees all over the world are hurting. Between hurricanes, fires, infestations, indiscriminate logging, and climate change our trees need extra amounts of care and love. Celebrating trees helps us to raise our own consciousness, as well as those around us. When we become more aware of the trees and what they need to be healthy, our connection grows ever stronger. And the trees do respond.

I believe that many of the passages about trees are very old ones that were incorporated into the Biblical library of books. Their original messages were probably too popular for the emerging priesthood to ignore or remove, so they sought to hide them either by verbiage or through translations.

Deut 20:19 is one such passage that was likely inserted into a wartime tale. The discussion surrounding the passage is what to do (or not) in the case of a "siege of war." The people are admonished not to cut down the trees . . . "for the tree of the field is man's life." It's odd that the Bible should suddenly be so concerned with "man's life" when two passages before in Deut 20:17 the discussion is about the "complete destruction" of other cultures in the area; the Hittites, Amorites, Canaanites, Perizzites, Hivites, and Jebusites.

The passage itself is three words: *Ha-adam ets hassadeh. Ets,* as we have seen, means tree. *Adam* is obvious because it's also a familiar name, and *hassadeh* is the land or fields. We've seen *Adam* in relation to trees and food before in the Bible and that, of course, didn't turn out so well. It is ironic that the grand deity, who had once punished Adam for eating the fruit of the trees is now advocating for that very thing. There is some confusion of message which is why I consider this passage to be quite old. It seems to be a blend of older and newer stories.

EXPERIENCING THE VIBRATIONAL ESSENCES

One of my teachers, Serge Kahili King who is Kumu Kupua (founder and leader) of Aloha International, the author of *Urban Shaman* and many other books, once taught a lesson. He asked who wanted to learn how to speak to trees. We all raised our hands in excitement thinking we would learn a great secret. He waved his hand at the nearest tree and said, "Hi tree." And so it is. The great secret is no secret at all, but what we are taught over and over and that is how connected we all are. Because we are so connected, simple communication works. Just a simple, "hi tree" creates a recognition which is a bridge of interaction that nourishes us.

Mantra

You can use this mantra: *Ha-adam ets hassadeh.*
Or you can just repeat *ets.*
Or speak your own words of love.

Mudra and Mandala

The mudra is to put your hands on the tree. Celebrate each tree. Hug the trees. Chant to the trees. Send them love. Water the trees with water/wine/juice that you have blessed.

The mandala is the tree itself. As in the previous section, use what resources you have when working with this practice.

Chapter 12 – Gratitude and Praise
Psalms 92:1, 100:4, 50:23, and 118:24

Psalm 92:1

A Psalm *or* Song for the sabbath day. *It is a* good *thing* to give thanks unto the LORD, and to sing praises unto thy name, O most High:
KJV

Songs of praises for this day of reverence. Flow with harmony, give thanks and blessings to Great Mystery, chant the holy name, YaaaHaaaVaaaHaaa.
MPV

Psalm 100:4

Enter into his gates with thanksgiving, *and* into his courts with praise: be thankful unto him, *and* bless his name.
KJV

Enter thresholds, be energized, embody sacred vibrations: do so
with thanksgiving, praise, and blessings.
MPV

Psalm 50:23

Whoso offereth praise glorifieth me: and to him that ordereth *his*
conversation *aright* will I shew the salvation of God.
KJV

Those who sacrifice thank offerings honor me, and to the
blameless I will show my salvation.
NIV

All-Potential, as Great Mystery, vibrates joy when given thank-
offerings, for this is the sacred quest of the heart.
MPV

Psalm 118:24

This *is* the day *which* the LORD hath made; we will rejoice and
be glad in it.
KJV

This day is filled with the essence of Great Mystery. Be with
ecstasy and rejoice.
MPV

COMMENTARY

The Book of Psalms is known as *Tehilim* in Hebrew or "song of praises." *Tehilim* comes from the same root as *hallelujah*. Another meaning from the same root is "shining as a star."[31] Praises are shining examples of how to live. Blessings, praise and thanksgiving are all of the same cloth. It is worth noting that the editors chose to leave an entire book of such praises in the Bible. In fact, praises, blessings and thanksgiving are the staples of religions throughout the world.

The sacred book of Hinduism, the Riga Veda is a text of sacred lore praising old gods. The term *rigveda*[32] itself means "praise knowledge."

St. Francis of Assisi's Canticle of Brother Sun and Sister Moon begins, "Most High, all-powerful, all-good Lord, All praise is Yours, all glory, all honour and all blessings."

The word *Eucharist,* the Christian sacrament, comes from a Greek word meaning "thankfulness" or "gratitude."

In Islam the oft used term *Alhamdulillah* means Praise Be to Allah.

The Haudenosaunee begin their Thanksgiving Address "Today we have gathered and we see that the cycles of life continue. We have been given the duty to live in balance and harmony with each other and all living things. So now, we bring our minds together as one as we give greetings and thanks to each other as people. Now our minds are one."[33]

The Bible, too, has a tradition of giving thanks.

---

[31] Benner 103.

[32] https://www.etymonline.com/word/Rig%20veda (consulted 11/30/25). The *rg* root also means to shine or radiate.

[33] This address is used by the Haudenosaunee (Iroquois Confederacy) to open and close major gatherings or meetings. The prayer is also by individuals to mark the beginning or end of the day. It is said to be over 1000 years old.

Psalm 92:1

The word "good" or *tov* figures prominently here. It is reminiscent of Genesis when the world is being created, and God declares it is "good." Based on its original meaning, Jeff A Benner translates *tov* as functional. I like his translation, but it still holds onto the dualistic aspect by implication. When something is good, our minds tend to think about how something else, generally its opposite, is "bad."

I translate *tov* as "functional harmony," because it means all is working or flowing together as designed. *Tov* represents harmony with function.

Psalm 100:4

Thresholds are important because they are the borderlands. They are the realms where we can move between worlds through portals, doors or gateways. Thresholds are the spaces of magic which nourish moments of transformation. The beach is one such space where the watery world of the ocean meets the sandy (or rocky) world of land. Other such spaces include labyrinths, standing stone circles, and eddies where salt and fresh water meet. Truly we ourselves are thresholds. For more on thresholds, see Jacob's story in chapters 15 and 16 and the appendix on mystery schools.

Psalm 50:23

My MPV translation for this passage is especially divergent. I love the "thank offerings" of the NIV but I am not sure why such a gifting would be seen as a sacrifice. Then I remembered one of the roots of sacrifice – "to make sacred." Sacer in Latin means "holy." Such a gifting does add to the sacredness.

The "I will shew" from the KVJ indicates a revealing or an opening, possibly a vision. The word for "ordereth," in the KJV and "blameless" in the NIV can also mean "road" or "wholeness." Together, they indicate a questioning that gives rise to a quest.

Although "heart" isn't specifically cited in the Hebrew, the words do indicate "glorious" and even "delight." These adjectives are foundational to an opening of the heart.

EXPERIENCING THE VIBRATIONAL ESSENCES

Mantra

This is an excellent opportunity to use yaaa-haaa-vaaa-haaa, the translation for LORD, in a chant. This is part of a larger chant called the *tseruf* from Abraham Abulafia, a 12th century Jewish kabbalist (see Appendix 1). *Tseruf* means "transformation." There is a reason these syllables have stood the test of time, they are powerful, and they connect our earth-based physical bodies with the divine nature of the heavens. In this way, our own bodies actualize a threshold space.

Mandala

Picture in your mind's eye that which fills your heart with love.

Mudra

Blessing hands with palms open and outward or upward. The focus is to have the hands open so the energy of the palms can be activated in this pose. Following are two examples.

This unique and beautifully preserved figurine was one of the first Greek experiments in casting the female form in bronze. She may have been a votive offering, possibly to the goddess Artemis between 675 and 650 BCE.

This file was provided to Wikimedia Commons by the Walters Art Museum as part of a cooperation project.

Coatlicue (Nahuatl as "Rock of the snake," Aztec earth goddess) statue from Coxcatlán, Puebla, shown in the National Museum of Anthropology, Mexico City Photo by Anagoria, Wikimedia Commons. ca 1500.

Chapter 13 – A Study in Praise

Psalm 150: 1-6

Psalm 150: 1-6

1) Praise ye the LORD. Praise God in his sanctuary: praise him in the firmament of his power.
2) Praise him for his mighty acts: praise him according to his excellent greatness.
3) Praise him with the sound of the trumpet: praise him with the psaltery and harp.
4) Praise him with the timbrel and dance: praise him with stringed instruments and organs.
5) Praise him upon the loud cymbals: praise him upon the high sounding cymbals.
6) Let every thing that hath breath praise the LORD. Praise ye the LORD.
KJV

1) Praise YaaaHaaaVaaaHaaa, praise divinity with all that is sacred, praise divinity who forged life's generative vigor from out of the fires of the firmament.

2) Praise YaaaHaaaVaaaHaaa, the abundant outflowing of great
mystery.
3) Praise YaaaHaaaVaaaHaaa using trumpet, psaltery and harp.
4) Praise YaaaHaaaVaaaHaaa with timbrel and dance, strings and
flute.
5) Praise YaaaHaaaVaaaHaaa using loud cymbals in the midst of
rejoicing.
6) All spirit/breath.beings sing with praise YaaaHaaaVaaaHaaa.
MPV

1) Hal-lu-ya, hal-lu-el, hal-lu-hu.
2) Hal-lu-hu, hal-lu-hu
3) Hal-lu-hu, hal-lu-hu
4) Hal-lu-hu, hal-lu-hu
5) Hal-lu-hu, hal-lu-hu
6) Hal-lel-ya, Hal-lu-ya
**The Hebrew syllables of praise in each passage (with the
other words stripped out.)**

COMMENTARY

The KJV word for "strength" in Psalm 150:1 is *oz* (phonetic *oze* or *ohz)*. (Strong's 5797) Fabre d'Olivet translates this word into the wonderfully descriptive phrase; "generative vigor."[34]

This is a fundamental energy that drives creation, a type of sexual energy. It is not sexuality per se but the procreative vigor that is generative fuel, the driving vitality behind creation.

Oze story: *I have had the privilege of twice attending assemblies led by the Reverend William Barber II. He has ankylosing spondylitis, a crippling form of rheumatoid arthritis that leaves him hunched over and in pain. Both times when I witnessed him, he approached the stage walking gingerly with a cane. Both times, I thought to myself, oh my, he doesn't look well. But when he began speaking, he was transformed. Not only did he stand on his feet for well over an hour, but he preached with such vigor that everyone in the audience was stirred by the waves of energy he was emitting. It was an astonishing metamorphosis. He is inspiring on so many levels. This, to me, is a true example of the generative vigor of oz.*

In the third set of Psalm 150, I have written out only the Hebrew hal-la-hu's and their variations. I have stripped out the other words of the passage so the reader can savor the original Hebrew. In this manner, one can dive into the cadences and rhythms of these words of praise.

As we saw in Chapter 1, *hallelujah* is a major vibrational pattern that reverberates through our bodies and connects us to spirit work. The word itself means praise *ya.* with *ya* being shorthand for the holy name YHVH.[35] There is further depth ni this passage: Hal-lu-ya, hal-lu-el, hal-lu-hu. The literal translation of this phrasing is – praise Ya, praise El and praise HU.

---

[34] d'Olivet, 416
[35] http://en.wikipedia.org/wiki/*Hallelujah*; consulted September 2012.

EXPERIENCING THE VIBRATIONAL ESSENCES

Mantra

This is an excellent opportunity to use *hallelujah* as a chant.
There are two main pronunciations:
HA-LA-LU-YA
AH-LA-LU-YA
Ah-la-lu-ya is written in some sources as Alleluya. Phonetically is it ahhh-laaa-luuu-yaaa.

Another chant that is very powerful follows the first line praises from the Psalm:
HAL-LU-YA, HAL-LU-EL, HAL-LU-HU.

Or you can also do the full six lines of the praises from the psalm. *Hallelujah* and YaaaHaaaVaaaHaaa have similar vibrational essences

Mandala and Mudra

I recommend using the mandala and mudra from the previous chapter.

Chapter 14 – Mystical Journeys

Psalm 148:13 and Psalms 93:1-5

En-chant-ment
Definition: the state of being under the influence of magic.[36]

Psalm 148:13

Let them praise the name of the LORD:
for this name alone is excellent;
glory above the earth and heaven.
KJV

Praise and celebrate the vibrations of YaaaHaaaVaaaHaaa:
open the veils of splendor which interweave the earth and the
heavens.
MPV

---

[36] Definition from the Cambridge On-Line Dictionary. Special: thanks to
David Elkington for making this connection.

Psalm 93:1

The LORD reigneth, he is clothed with majesty; the LORD is
clothed with strength, *wherewith* he hath girded himself: the
world also is stablished, that it cannot be moved.
KJV

Vibration.Being danceth uniting divinity and earth in generative
vigor adorned by soil and stars. Thus is the abundant flow of
seeds set in perpetual cyclic motion.
MPV

Psalm 93:2

Thy throne *is* established of old: thou *art* from everlasting.
KJV

Thy vibration floweth into and through the space of time
blessing time-laden seed.beings in their everlasting cycles.
MPV

Psalm 93:3

The floods have lifted up, O LORD, The floods have lifted up
their voice;
The floods lift up their waves.
KJV

The light infused seed.beings dance oh Vibration.Being, the light
infused seed.beings roar thunder;

The light infused seed.beings burst forth with life.
MPV

Psalm 93:4

The LORD on high *is* mightier Than the noise of many waters,
Than the mighty waves of the sea.
KJV

Vibration.Being roars, shepherding gushing waters through
thresholds,
midwifing creation from heaven, midwifing creation from earth,
midwifing creation from heaven/earth.
MPV

Psalm 93:5

Thy testimonies are very sure: holiness becometh thine house,
O LORD, for ever.
KJV

Witnesses of devotion, holiness of indwelling,
Great Mystery oh, time blending with timelessness, enduringly.
MPV

COMMENTARY

I put Psalm 148:13 together with Psalms 93:1-5. Each of these passages expresses mystical experiences and journeys in a poetic and Biblical fashion.

Psalm: 148:13

In KJV version the name LORD is deemed "excellent." This is an example of why I use YaaaHaaaVaaaHaaa as it exhibits one of those "excellencies" that this name entails. It is an experiential opportunity to feel, vibrate, explore, and celebrate this holy name. The name is "excellent" because when we speak it, we can feel it in our bodies and in our bones. This passage also talks about the "veils" between the worlds. In Genesis when God is separating out the opposites, the doors or veils between the worlds remain open and this is one of the keys to otherworldly or mystical experiences

Psalm 93: often titled, The Lord Reigns

Typical commentary of Psalm 93 speaks to the power of "God" which can be seen in the KJV translations where divinity is compared to royalty and kingship by using such words as "reign," "majesty," and "throne."

The Hebrew words reveal a whole other side to this powerful Psalm which I liken to the "beauty of the divine" rather than the more traditional, "the lord reigns." Vibration.Being, Great Mystery, and Mother/Father Creator all have the AWE-inspiring ability to midwife creation and birth. In other words, to make love manifest.

Psalm 93 is an esoteric poem bursting with motion that begins by creating an eco-system (Earth) for life to exist. This poem is filled with sound vibrations, thunderous surf, the movement of water and descriptions of thresholds. As the motion unfolds, one is invited to participate in the powerful energies of the divine pouring out through these threshold gateways.

Psalm 93:1

The KJV word for "strength" is *oz* as we saw in the previous chapter. D'Olivet translates this word as "generative vigor."

The word for "established" is *tikkun* (Strong's 359). Readers may know this word from the phrase *tikkun olam* which means to repair the world. It is built upon the word *kun* which Benner refers to as the "opening of a seed."[37] I think of it as both the "opening" and the "blessing of the seeds." We see over and over, but hidden, how important seeds are in the establishment of life on the Earth.

The word for "world" in this passage is *tebel* (Strong's 8398) which is formed from the letters "bl" which Benner translates as "a flowing."[38] Again we get the concept of movement.

Psalm 93:2

A throne in pagan times often meant the "lap of the Goddess."[39] I use seed.beings to put it into juxtaposition to *humanity.being* (human being) and Vibration.Being. Both words from the phrase *tikkun [as kun]* and *olam* appear in this passage. For this reason, I bring in the concept of seeds into my translation.

---

[37] Benner, 149.
[38] Benner, 66.
[39] The Goddess name Isis comes from the Egyptian word for throne. https://www.britannica.com/topic/Isis-Egyptian-goddess (consulted 11/30/2025)

Psalm 93:3

Nahar (Strong's 5104) is the word translated to "floods." We can go back to Chapter 8 (Genesis 2:10 and Psalm 36:8) which discusses how flowing, in this case, overflowing water carries seeds.

The root of *nahar* is N-H-R which Benner describes as "the life giving water that washes over the soil."[40] Benner also notes that the basic root NR means "seed beginning."[41] D'Olivet writes: "[It] constitutes a root whose purpose is to characterize that which propagates light . . . A lamp, a beacon, a torch: a sage, a guide; that which enlightens, shines, is radiant. . ."[42]

The word for "voice" is *qol* (Strong's 6963) which Benner describes as "the sound of the shepherd, musical instrument, the wind, thunder, etc . ."[43]

The word for wave is *doki* (Strong's 1796). Benner describes it this way: "Seeds are placed in a stone mortar, a stone cup, the stone pestle is moved around the cup to crush the seeds into a powder." With this definition, we see that the wave action does the threshing that allows the seeds to burst forth with life. Waves are interesting as they operate in places of thresholds, the joining of land and water where the two meet and interact.

Psalm 93: 4

The word for noise we saw in Psalm 93:3 is *qol.* It is a sound filled with all noises. For more context we can look back to Chapters 6 and 7 about Joyful Noise and the Divine as Music and their role in creation.

This passage uses a different word for waves: *mishbar* (Strong's 4867). It indicates large waves breaking on shore. This

---

[40] Benner, 190.
[41] Ibid.
[42] d'Olivet, 404.
[43] Benner, 245.

is what Benner writes: "The grain is placed on the threshing floor or in the millstone and crushed to burst out seeds from the hulls."[44]

So even though the wording is different, the theme we saw in 93:3 carries on. Another related word is "birth canal" which Benner describes as "the place of bursting through."[45] This is an interesting description of human birth.

Psalm 93: 5

The word for holy used in this passage is *quadosh* with its erotic connotations which I discussed in chapter 7.

As so often described, noise sets up the vibration that solidifies into the manifestation of life. The noise is associated with, and moves through, water or *mayim*, the great mysterious mother waters.

---

[44] Benner, 452.
[45] Ibid.

Chapter 15 – Jacob's Ladder part 1, Dreamtime

Genesis 28:11 through 28:15

For this chapter and the next, I am including the commentary directly after each individual passage in order to break out the elements of the shamanic rite/experience that is described.

Genesis 28:11

And he lighted upon a certain place, and tarried there all night, because the sun was set; and he took of the stones of that place, and put *them for* his pillows, and lay down in that place to sleep.
KJV

And when he came to a threshold place at a threshold time, Jacob did rituals of honoring; then, in loving communion, he laid upon Mother Earth and entered dreamtime.
MPV

<u>**COMMENTARY**</u>

The hallmark of a quest is to travel from the known into the unknown. It can be either a physical journey or one of dreamtime, a vision. Jacob does both.

Jacob is an active participant in this unfolding drama. Thresholds are considered gateways or doorways between elements, realms or different worlds. Jacob has landed in a threshold place. How do we know this? The word used is *maqom* (Strong's 4725). *Maqom* is used to represent a sacred place where the spiritual veils are thin, and revelations are often revealed.

Jacob was also there at a threshold time. There are the four times of the day that are considered to be thresholds; dawn, dusk, noon and midnight. Jacob is there at dusk, which we know because of the mention of the sun having set.

The word used when Jacob lies down is *shakab* (Strong's 7901). This word implies that the lying down is for sexual relations. In this case we can think of the word as expressing passion and rising of energies which are the essential fuels that propel the quest for a vision.

<u>**Genesis 28:12**</u>

And he dreamed, and behold a ladder set up on the earth, and the top of it reached to heaven: and behold the angels of God ascending and descending on it.
KJV

Jacob entered the liminal dreamtime where the threshold veils were pierced. A pathway was revealed to which Jacob responded, "I am here." He could see the energetic currents of creation, the workings of All-Potential cycling between heaven and earth.
MPV

As Jacob dreams, he sees a vision of a ladder, a common shamanic symbol for traveling between otherworldly landscapes. A tree is another symbol that serves the same function. They are conduits that allow shamans and others to travel amidst the realms.

Hinneh (Strong's 2009) is a powerful word that means behold and is used to mean "pay attention." It is also used to indicate that divine revelation is at hand.

This word is also used in a slightly different form in other crucial moments of divine interactions. The variation is *hineni* which is *hinneh* plus *ani. Ani* means "I." *Hineni* means "I am here." *Hinneh* means "here." This is the state of being fully present and a participant to the mysteries that are about to unfold. In Genesis 22:1 (and two other times) Abraham answers *hineni* when divinity calls. Moses says *hineni* in Exodus 3:4 when he is called from the Burning Bush.

The Hebrew in the text of Jacob's story is *hinneh,* not *hineni.* Nevertheless, I felt "I am here" is an appropriate translation for several reasons. This was Jacob's personal experience which only he could have told in the original "I" perspective. From a spiritual point of view, he was present and participating in the mysteries that he experienced in communication with the divine.

The term used for the top of the ladder is *rosh* or head (Strong's 7218). This is the same root of the word "in the beginning" in Genesis 1:1. The literal meaning in Genesis 1:1 is at the head or headwaters. The use of this same word gives the sense that what Jacob is seeing is not only divine but is a peek into the secrets of creation.

Naga (Strong's 5060) is to touch. The touch of the divine can be destructive or revelatory. Such a "touch" carries energy, power and knowledge. People react differently, it can burn, it can smite but it can also be ecstatic and filled with wisdom.

Genesis 28:13

And, behold, the LORD stood above it, and said, I *am* the LORD
God of Abraham thy father, and the God of Isaac: the land
whereon thou liest, to thee will I give it, and to thy seed;
KJV

Witness, Great Mystery. Here in this place, Behold. The
passageways, from heaven to earth, from your ancestors to your
descendants. You belong to the many-seeded Cauldron of Source.
MPV

COMMENTARY

When one enters such a liminal space, the mysterious
becomes manifest. That can take many forms such as a vision, an
experience, or a speaking voice. How this appears can have as
many varieties as there are people in the world. Elements of this
experience can be seen as aspects of divinity, ancestors, possibly
seeds representing fertility and growth. Because Jacob announced
his presence, *hineni*, he was expressing that he was available to
have this visionary experience. The text and traditional translations
speak about Jacob's direct ancestors, Abraham and Isaac. I chose
to make the ancestral links more general and thus nongendered.

Genesis 28:14

And thy seed shall be as the dust of the earth, and thou shalt
spread abroad to the west, and to the east, and to the north, and to
the south: and in thee and in thy seed shall all the families of the
earth be blessed.
KJV

Blessings to the four directions of time/space to manifest *humanity.beings* and to set in place the cauldron which protects, nourishes, blesses and disperses the seeds of life throughout the Earth.
MPV

COMMENTARY

Hu, as seen in <u>hu</u>man being or *<u>hu</u>manity.beings*, is a power syllable that has been used to indicate divinity in all corners of the world, Celtic, Mayan, Egyptian, Judaic, Christian, to name a few.[46] Our own designation is that we are human beings confirming our connection to the divine. Humanity is a broad word. In many shamanic systems the word itself refers to all of creation, not just human life.

When we think about the grand mystery of creation, it is a numinous concept that is devoid of time, space, duality, and manifestation. In order for us to have a home, a place to exist, a land of time/space leading to duality/manifestation needed to be "carved" out. When we think of our Mother Earth in these terms, we come to appreciate just how special and precious this world is. Its edges are mapped out by the four directions as well as the four elements of earth, air, fire and water.

---

[46] The sound of HU was one of the names of the Egyptian sphinx. <u>Hu</u>nab Ku of the Mayans was the god at the heart of creation. A<u>shu</u>ku is a syllable of wisdom from Buddhism. A<u>hu</u>ra Mazda is a being of light wisdom from Persia. Hu is the all-encompassing ruling deity of the Celtics and husband to Ceridwen. Yesh-hu-ah the Aramaic name for Jesus contains hu. One of the more traditional pronunciations of YHVH – ya-hu-ah also contains hu. The HU sounds connect humanity to the divine.

<u>**Genesis 28:15**</u>

And, behold, I *am* with thee, and will keep thee in all *places* whither thou goest, and will bring thee again into this land; for I will not leave thee, until I have done *that* which I have spoken to thee of.
KJV

Behold, as long as *ehyeh* breathes in time/space, these manifest passageways will endure for knowledge, interchange, energy, wisdom, life. And my cauldron of seeds will continue.
MPV

<u>**COMMENTARY**</u>

It is common to communicate with spirit as divinity or a guide. In this passage, divinity and humanity are coming together with the promise that life and seeds will continue.

EXPERIENCING THE VIBRATIONAL ESSENCES

Mantra

Hineni, I am here!

Mandala

A tree. Think of the energy of the tree. Sap rising. Leaves emerging, green leaves, fall leaves. Squirrels climbing. Birds nesting. Bees droning.

You can also use a ladder as your image or any aspect that spans the space between the earth and the skies. Rainbow, clouds, a plant rising up from the soil. Stairway. A visualization of your own spine as the conduit between heaven and earth.

Mudra

The intent of the posture is to focus on empowerment along with openness for whatever experiences come our way. Think open-hearted empowerment.

Feel free to experiment with empowerment poses including ones already used. Below are three examples of one pose that has been used for millennia. This is a power pose. Stand straight with hands on hips. Following you can see it used from an ancient sculpture to a sports icon to a superhero.

Goddess on the Throne – terracotta figurine found close to Prishtina, Kosovo – on display in the Kosovo Museum The seated terracotta figure measures 18.5 cm high and is dated to 5700–4500 BCE. Photo by Albinfo, Wikimedia Commons.

Johnny Valentine, 1970 Wikimedia Commons, public domain.

Statue of actress Lynda Carter as Wonder Woman, beautiful plaster series. Photo by Rob Olivera, Wikimedia Commons.

Chapter 16 – Jacob's Ladder, part 2, Awakening
Genesis 28:16 to 28:19

Genesis 28:16

And Jacob awaked out of his sleep, and he said, Surely the LORD is in this place; and I knew *it* not.
KJV

And Jacob awakened to a new day, and he said, Surely Great Mystery filters through everything and everyone and I understood it not. And yet it is in this sacred place that I learned.
MPV

COMMENTARY

After such an experience, it is time to integrate it into our lives. Most mythic stories talk about this happening in an instant. And while certainly possible, it is not uncommon for the process to take many years, even decades. The process involves first recognizing that something mystical or otherworldly happened. This is what Jacob does when he talks about god/the divine/great mystery occurring at that place.

Genesis 28:17

And he was <u>afraid,</u> and said, How <u>dreadful</u> *is* this place! this *is* none other but the house of God, and this *is* the gate of heaven.
KJV

He was <u>afraid</u> and said, "How <u>awesome</u> is this place! This is none other than the house of God; this is the gate of heaven."
NIV

And he <u>trembled</u> and said, how <u>inspirited</u> is this place, for earth is the dwelling place of All-Potential and it is here that I found a gateway.
MPV

COMMENTARY

Fear, awe, trembling can all indicate that an experience of power and spirit is afoot. Trembling is often the way we feel the movement of spirit within our bodies. It can indicate an experience of mysticism and generative energy flow. The traditional passages speak of Jacob being fearful. The New International version, while speaking of fear, also uses the term awesome. I pair the words tremble and inspirited.

The Hebrew word that is translated as both afraid and awesome in the NIV and as afraid and dreadful in the KJV are both the same; *yare* (S 3372*)*. At its most basic, *yare* means fluid or flowing (the idea is that when we are afraid, our insides will turn watery).

In English we also have this grouping of words that, with slight changes, mean apparent opposites; awesome/awful; terrific/terrible, fearsome/fearful.

The feelings of great fear and great ecstasy can feel the same in our bodies at any given moment, a wellspring of flowing energy. It is the reason that John Mellencamp and others can sing the very relatable lyrics "it hurts so good."[47]

God-fearing has been used as a compliment. Fear as something to strive for is a tension creating force. It is a constricted form of energy flow. I think it is more of a compliment to say Great Mystery-aweing (or more traditionally God-aweing).

Genesis 28:18-19

And Jacob rose up early in the morning,
and took the stone that he had put for his pillows,
and set it up for a pillar, and poured oil upon the top of it.
And he called the name of that place Bethel:
but the name of that city was called Luz at the first.
KJV

And Jacob arose at dawn from his dream-time
and took the earth and stone which had cradled him in his journey
through the veil, and created an altar. He poured libations of oil
onto the altar.
And spoke aloud the name, Bethel or House of All-Potential
which was once known as Luz, the light from the Tree of Life.
MPV

COMMENTARY

It is considered good spirit etiquette to honor important experiences in our lives. It is also the second aspect in the process of integrating deep spiritual messages into our lives. Jacob takes the stones and sets them up as an altar or sacred space. He anoints them with oil.

---

[47] Other singers include Millie Jackson and Astrid S.

He then renames the place Beth-El. Beth is an alternative spelling of *beyt* and means house and El is the divine name which I translate as All-Potential.

The place was already special as it had been called *Luz*. *Luz* in the Latin languages means light. While it does not have this specific meaning in Hebrew, it is connected with light. For more information on the connection of light and *luz* in Hebrew, please see Appendix 3.

EXPERIENCING THE VIBRATIONAL ESSENCES

Mantra

Yare can be used as a mantra: yar-ayyyy. Use it to tap into the flowing energy. Think of it as plugging into an electric socket that is streaming with energy or otherwise being in the flow of harmony.

Mandala

The inspiration for this mandala comes from an ancient Pyramid text from the Third dynasty (2686-2613 BCE). It states

> *. . .a stairway to the sky is set up for you among the Imperishable Stars[48]*

In discussing this image, Corinne Heline writes: "Upon the ladder of the spine the life forces both descend and ascend, flowing through the central canal of the spinal cord as a stream of light."[49]

The mandala for this chant is a staircase, a ladder or your own spinal cord with flowing light streaming through it.

Mudra

Hold hands in front of your sternum. Left over right with the fingers draping as they do in the statuettes following. Leave space between palms for air flow.

---

[48] *Pyramid Text* From Djoser's pyramid, Third dynasty (2686-2613 BCE) [quoted in Billard, *Pyramids: Building for Eternity* by IES Edwards, 78.]
[49] Corine Heline, *The Bible and The Tarot,* DeVorss Publications, 1969, 110.

Standing female worshiper ca. 2600–2500 BCE. Sumerian woman, The Metropolitan Museum of Art, Wikimedia commons, public domain.

This statuette and the previous one are from the City-State of Ur in the time of Enheduanna who was a priestess of Istar/Inanna. Photo my own, taken at the Morgan Library Museum.

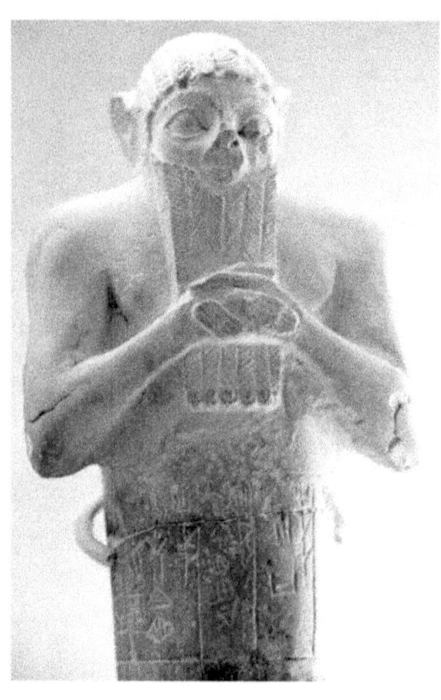

Limestone foundation peg of Lugal-kisal-si, the King of Uruk and Ur. From the temple of goddess Nammu (also Namma) at Uruk, Iraq. Early Dynastic period, c. 2380 BCE. Pergamon Museum, Berlin, Germany.
Photo by Osama Shukir Muhammed Amin FRCP(Glasg) Wikimedia Commons.

Personal experience: *I was working on this book in the hot days of summer. To take a break, one day when the skies were cloudy and there was a nice breeze, I decided to go on a bike ride. I was out pretty far out when suddenly the clouds cleared, the wind died down and the air became sultry and uncomfortable. As I turned toward home, I was already panting and feeling the pressure of the now humid, and heavy air. About ½ way back I wasn't sure I could make it without some help. I started chanting yar-ayyyy, at first out loud and then quietly like a bee buzzing. I couldn't hold a mudra as my hands were on the handlebars and I couldn't focus on a mandala since I was cycling on streets. But it turns out that chanting yare was sufficient. I had done the chant enough so that my body knew the patterns and it settled into a "flow mode." I made it home, wilted but safe.*

Chapter 17 – Abraham And Isaac

Genesis 22:1-11

Note: The format of this chapter is different. The story of Abraham's willingness to sacrifice Isaac has been written about through many distinct angles. The point of view of this writing is through shamanic eyes with a view to how such pagan ceremonies were performed. I will begin with the KJV version of the story. Then I will discuss the passages and compare them to the scholarly writings of Mircea Eliade who studied many shamanic systems throughout the world. In Commentary 1, I will share my translation that comes from these understandings. In Commentary 2, I write about Ismael, also Abraham's son, and his potential participation in this ritual.

Genesis 22:1-11

22:1 And it came to pass after these things, that God did tempt Abraham, and said unto him, Abraham: and he said, Behold, *here* I *am*.

22:2 And he said, Take now thy son, thine only *son* Isaac, whom thou lovest, and get thee into the land of Moriah; and offer him there for a burnt offering upon one of the mountains which I will tell thee of.

22:3 And Abraham rose up early in the morning, and saddled his ass, and took two of his young men with him, and Isaac his son, and clave the wood for the burnt offering, and rose up, and went unto the place of which God had told him.

22:4 Then on the third day Abraham lifted up his eyes, and saw the place afar off.

22:5 And Abraham said unto his young men, Abide ye here with the ass; and I and the lad will go yonder and worship, and come again to you.

22:6 And Abraham took the wood of the burnt offering, and laid *it* upon Isaac his son; and he took the fire in his hand, and a knife; and they went both of them together.

22:7 And Isaac spake unto Abraham his father, and said, My father: and he said, Here *am* I, my son. And he said, Behold the fire and the wood: but where *is* the lamb for a burnt offering?

22:8 And Abraham said, My son, God will provide himself a lamb for a burnt offering: so they went both of them together.

22:9 And they came to the place which God had told him of; and Abraham built an altar there, and laid the wood in order, and bound Isaac his son, and laid him on the altar upon the wood.

22:10 And Abraham stretched forth his hand, and took the knife to slay his son.

22:11 And the angel of the LORD called unto him out of heaven, and said, Abraham, Abraham: and he said, Here *am* I.
KJV

COMMENTARY 1 – Isaac

The Biblical story where Abraham sets off to sacrifice Isaac is enigmatic. It feels cruel on its surface but has many threads of ancient pagan ritual that peek through the storytelling.

Mystical writers describe many possibilities for the experience of being in the presence of an otherworldly essence. These essences can be guardian angels, deities, or spirits of any kind. It is not like sitting down with your friend at a bistro. It is, by definition, mystical, an experience that pierces the mists of the veils of the worlds. Deities and mystical figures are notorious for uttering riddles and other obscure communications. Although some people have reported "speaking" words with divinity, most such communication involves some kind of translation. That can be in the form of unraveling a riddle, hearing a sound we interpret as words, or seeing a mysterious visual that needs to be deciphered. We are still translating the meanings of divine interactions in the Bible to this day.

In that vein, how was Abraham so sure of the divine instruction that he was willing to kill his own son? Abraham hinges a lot on a correct interpretation of "God's will."

And why would an all-powerful deity even want to put a parent in that position? The Biblical story suggests that a god-figure is testing Abraham's obedience no matter the price. That begs another question. Why would Abraham be loyal to such a cruel god in the first place?

This same story appears in the Qur'an with some changes. In the Biblical story, Abraham is instructed to sacrifice Isaac, his "only" son. Since Ishmael was born first, Isaac was never Abraham's "only son." Even though Isaac is mentioned by name, Muslims infer that this story is about Hagar's son. In their telling it is Ishmael who faces sacrifice. Since murdering one's own child would not normally be considered virtuous, I began to wonder why two major religious systems are arguing for their son to be the one who is sacrificed. There must be other layers of meaning here.

What if, instead of a tale of Abraham's blind obedience, the core of this tale is his son's own vision quest with Abraham, the elder of the tribe, leading the youth through the process? This would make sense because this was a valued ritual in indigenous cultures. It was both a puberty ritual and conferred power on an individual.

We don't have the full extent of Isaac and Abraham's ceremony as it is abridged in the Biblical telling. It is even shorter in the Qur'an. But we do have the structure of the stories and both have the hallmarks of pagan rituals. This story is told about a male child. Most of the indigenous rituals that have been preserved also speak about the male child. For that reason, I will also use male markers in my telling.

Below are the 4 steps of a puberty rite of passage that follow the general teachings of a mystery school and can also be seen in the initiations of a shaman. For a further discussion of mystery schools and their teachings please see Appendix 4.

University of Chicago professor Mirea Eliade wrote extensively about these rituals. I have included his observations from two of his books: 1) *Rites and Symbols of Initiation (Rites)*[50] and 2) *Shamanism.*[51]

Step 1

A young child is separated from his mother and the world as he had known it. There are many ways this can happen. The child can be "kidnapped" in the middle of the night or taken right

---

[50] Mircea Eliade, *Rites and Symbols of Initiation: The Mysteries of Birth and Rebirth,* Harper and Row. Originally published in 1958, 1965 edition, translated by Willard R. Trask.
[51] Mircea Eliade, *Shamanism: Archaic Techniques of Ecstasy*, Bollingen Series LXXVI, Princeton University Press, originally printed 1951. 1974 edition, translated by Willard R. Trask.

out of the mother's arms during the day. The mothers keen and cry for their "lost child." This play-acting creates the ritualistic circumstances where transformation, from child to man is possible. Scholars have seen it as a way to make a ritualistic distinction between the relationship of a mother to her young child as opposed to a mother and her adult child.

Eliade discusses how this can play out. "The break is made in such a way as to produce a strong impression both on the mothers and the novices . . .the novices die to childhood and the mothers have a foreboding that the boys will never again be what they were before initiation; *their* children . . . The very act of separation from their mothers fills them with forebodings of death – for they are seized by the unknown, often masked men, carried far from their familiar surroundings, laid on the ground, and covered with branches."[52]

Step 2

The elder, father, or guide of the community takes the boy on a journey quest that follows instructions given by spirit. They arrive at a sacred place or landscape. Abraham took Isaac to sacred learning grounds called Moriah.

Eliade discusses an Australian ceremony of puberty which is representative of the genre. "For the sacred ground is at once an image of the world (*imago mundi*) and a world sanctified by the presence of the Divine Being."[53]

Moriah is a word with no clear translation. Rashi (French rabbi, b. 1040) wrote one of my favorite uses of the term where he connects it to "teachers" and teaching. According to Strong's 4179, the term *moriah* is formed from two important words. *Yah* (3050) which is half the Tetragrammaton, the holy name. It signifies the divine. And *raah* (7200) which means to see, to behold, to have visions. This makes Moriah a place where one sees or has visions of the divine.

---

[52] Eliade, *Rites*, pps 8-9.
[53] Eliade, *Rites*, pg 6.

<u>**Step 3**</u>

A vision quest involves some amount of isolation. It can also include being physically stressed with bindings, piercings, along with deprivations such as fasting and being exposed to the elements. The ritual aspects are usually kept secret so the specific "how-to's" are only known to initiates. In general, these can involve ritual dismemberment, a dream or action of being stripped to one's bones as a symbolic death. Isaac is bound by Abraham, who in this case can be seen as his father, teacher, or elder. One purpose is to allow one's mind, or one's inner spirit to roam free while one's body is anchored to the Earth. It also symbolizes the cocoon as a container of transformation.

Eliade describes elements of the initiation. "Dream, sickness, or initiation ceremony, the central element is always the same: death and symbolic resurrection of the neophyte, involving a cutting up of the body performed in various ways (dismemberment, gashing, opening of the abdomen, etc . .)"[54]

There is often a display of ritual instruments. Although it is not specified how they are ultimately used, the elements of dismemberment (Abraham's knife) and of fire (the wood and references to the burnt offering) are present in the Biblical story.

Eliade discusses an Australian tribe which builds a fire as part of the ceremony and the novices are "roasted" with fire. This contains the same symbology as the burnt offering.[55]

Eliade also lays out who particularly would go through such a rite. For some cultures, it was general for all children, but it was specially used for those who have a "mystical vocation" such as shaman, medicine man or in this case, a son destined to become a religious patriarch.[56]

---

[54] Eliade, *Shamanism*, pg 56.
[55] Eliade, *Rites*, pg 7.
[56] Eliade, *Rites*, pps 2-3.

Personal Story: *In the mid 1990s I had a series of initiatory visions or dreams. They were one of the impetuses that led me to follow the path of the shaman. The visions lasted for 9 months and in the course of them, I experienced a repeating ritual of symbolic death. I made a tapestry of images from those dreams. This is in the lower right corner of that tapestry. It is a floret made up of images of bones, blood and a heart muscle. The baskets are there because my bones and sometimes my organs were placed in the baskets before a dream guide would come and help me to re-animate. Eventually in the course of these dreams I learned to do it myself. The processes became part of my shamanic training.*

<u>Step 4</u>

The final step involves rebirth, resurrection, and finally a return to the community changed. This can involve the intercession of an angel or a deity.

Eliade discusses this in several spots in his book *Shamanism.*

- pgs 36-37: An account of Yakut culture: "Here the shaman undergoes his initiation. The spirits cut off his head, which they set aside (for the candidate must watch his dismemberment with his own eyes), and cut him into small pieces, which are then distributed to the spirits of various diseases. Only by undergoing such an ordeal will the future shaman gain the power to cure. His bones are then covered with new flesh, and in some cases, he is given new blood."

- pg 38: "We find the central theme of an initiation ceremony: dismemberment of the neophyte's body and renewal of his organ; ritual death followed by resurrection."

- pg 69: " .. the majority of myths concerning the origin of shamans posit the direction intervention of God."

<u>Genesis 22:1 – 11</u>

22:1 In the fullness of time, Isaac grew from boyhood to the first blush of adulthood. And All-Potential spoke to Abraham, the elder of his tribe. "Hineni, here I am," answered Abraham.

22:2 It is time for Isaac to be initiated into the mysteries. Just as you and Sarah attended the Egyptian mystery school in your youth, it is now time for Isaac. Take Isaac from his mother and bring him to the sacred lands of Moriah, the sacred land for visions.

22:3) And Abraham took Isaac from his mother, gathered his tools and journeyed to the sacred teaching land just as he was instructed.

22:4) On the 3rd day, their eyes raised up to see the hallowed land which they were approaching.

22:5) Abraham said to his servants, "We are heading into sacred territory to enact the great mysteries which are secret and for initiates only. Stay here and we will return."

22:6) Abraham and Isaac gathered up the tools for their ritual and proceeded to the place of sacred teachings.

22:7) Isaac was fearful as is the way of initiates who face their ordeals. He had questions but they were not answered. He would find his own answers through the action of ceremony. They intoned the sacred word that marked the beginning of the rites: *Hineni.*

22:8-9) And at the sacred teaching grounds, Isaac was called to face his own death as part of the quest to understand the mysteries of life. As in the times of old, Isaac was bound with ropes, for this experience, his body was to be anchored so his visions could run free.

22:10) To prepare for his vision quest, Isaac was shown the knife that would be used for his ritual dismemberment. This was to presage the sacrifice, the moment to rise up and experience thresholds between worlds – a vision quest to seek out the mysteries of life and death.

22:11) Isaac was instructed that when he had experienced re-enfleshment, in other words, his rebirth, he was to call upon the angels to set him free from his fetters. And so it was.

Hineni: (Completion of the ritual) When the ritual was complete, Isaac rose at the call of the angels for he had completed his ordeal. Abraham answered hineni to indicate the completion.

Those, like Isaac, who go through mystery school training experiences and face the realities of their own deaths, emerge lighter, and happier for death is no longer feared. And Isaac grew into his name which translates to *laughter and joy*.
MPV

* * *

COMMENTARY 2 – Ishmael

It appears that Ishmael went through his own initiation or potential shamanic ceremony. The Biblical details are even more sparse than those of Isaac. We know there is communication through the thresholds as his mother, Hagar, speaks directly to God. In this case, she becomes the elder who leads the youth through the rituals rather than his father Abraham. There is the hint that Ishmael faces his own death experience.

Genesis 21:16
And she [Hagar] went, and sat her down over
against him a good way off,
as it were a bowshot: for she said,
Let me not see the death of the child.
And she sat over against him,
and lift up her voice, and wept.

And like Isaac, Ishmael was helped to be "lifted up" by angels after his ordeal where he is also laid out upon the land.

Genesis 21:17
And God heard the voice of the lad;
and the angel of God
called to Hagar out of heaven,
and said unto her,
What aileth thee, Hagar? fear not;
for God hath heard the voice of the lad where he is.

The text implies he is a baby but since Biblical stories are filled with time-bending elements it is possible that it is allegorical and represents a later time of vision seeking.

We don't know the content of either Isaac's or Ishmael's visions, but we do know that both became the leaders of their respective spiritual/religious pathways.

EXPERIENCING THE VIBRATIONAL ESSENCES

Begin this practice ceremonially by announcing HINENI.

Lie on the earth, as much as possible human skin to Earth skin. You can lie on your stomach or on your back. The mandala can either be Earth Herself or the sky with its expanse or perhaps a rainbow spanning both. Pay attention to the movements of clouds, leaves, branches etc . . . The mantra is not a sound but silence so you can be cognizant of the sounds of the earth. Be in the moment with each breath that you take.

Complete your practice by repeating HINENI.

Chapter 18 – Words, Womb and Wisdom

In the beginning was the Word, and the Word was with God,
and the Word was God.
John 1:1

This is the oft repeated quote from the Gospel of John. Many commentators, including myself, note that the Word is a form of vibration which harkens back to the beginning of Genesis

And the Spirit of God moved upon the face of the waters.
Genesis 1:2

As noted in Chapter 1, Matthew Fox has said "in the beginning was the energy." I love this as it expresses the concept of movement, spirit and vitality. As Fox notes, "a living word."

The Hebrew word for spirit is *ruach* which also means wind and breath, including the breath that we take as we speak. God is *Elohim* which I translate as "All Potential." Creation is all of one cloth. Divinity is breath. Breath is divinity, manifested on Earth or as John puts it "the Word."

Here are the lines of Genesis 1:2, just before the *ruach* of *Elohim* breaths upon the waters.

And the earth was without form, and void;

and darkness was upon the face of the deep.

The word for "deep" is *tehom* (Strong's 8415) which also means abyss and sea. *Tehom* is a key word in this passage. Etymologically, *tehom* and the name of the Babylonian Goddess Tiamat are related. [57] The use of the word *tehom* in Genesis is a remnant of the Great Sumerian Goddess of creation, reduced to a vocabulary word and then translated out of easy reach of the modern-day reader. Right there at the beginning of Creation, we have goddess energy. Think about how significant that is.

When we add in God's personal name: I AM that I AM, we get a very different perspective and a deep sense of how the feminine was hidden away within the Biblical words. As previously noted, there are two goddess names implicit within this personal name of God: Ashera and EVE.

Water is essentially a feminine element because it is the source of life. Goddesses connected with water are both creators of life and destroyers. One way to look at the concept of *tehom (face of the deep)* is that it refers to the dark, cold depths of the oceans that frighten us. And well they should. The oceanic cauldron is the source of creation, the formless abyss, undifferentiated oneness that contains all the raw materials for life. In the arc of evolution, life came out of the sea. The human fetus grows for nine months in the dark, watery womb of amniotic fluid. A seed is planted in the earth, needing both the darkness and the moisture of Mother Earth to grow. In our human form, we come from the source and we return to that same source — the cradle of oneness, the womb/tomb cauldron of the Great Mother Goddess.

The Sumerian creation story that discusses Tiamat is the Enuma Elish. Sumeria is one of the civilizations closest to Israel.

---

[57]Morris Jastrow, *Hebrew and Babylonian Traditions*, 2012 Forgotten Books (originally published by Scribner and Sons, 1914, 28 and Lewis Spence, *Myths & Legends of Babylonia & Assyria*, Forgotten Books, 2012 (originally published NY Frederick A Stokes Company, 1916), 72.

The Enuma Elish begins with Apsû, the god of subterranean sweet waters, and Tiamat as the goddess of the primeval saltwater ocean. The fresh waters of the god Apsû and the salt waters of the goddess Tiamat intermingle.

> *When on high the heaven had not been named,*
> *Firm ground below had not been called by name,*
> *Naught but primordial Apsû, their begetter,*
> *(And) Mummu-Tiamat, she who bore them all,*
> *Their waters commingling as a single body.*
> *Enuma Elish, 1ˢᵗ Tablet*[58]

The names Apsû and Tiamat are significant. Apsû is related to the word abyss and later came to mean "house of knowledge."[59] The abyss, that darkness of the deepest realms, is mythologically speaking, the primary source of knowledge, wisdom, and power here on Earth. The name Tiamat "epitomizes chaos,"[60] the chaos of that oceanic cauldron. It is the chaos of All-Potentiality.

When we consider the famous John quote alongside Genesis, what we have is Word or spirit/breath which mixes with the watery abyss or the womb of life in a potion that is filled with wisdom. Wisdom is a term that Cynthia Bourgeault uses in relation to the process. "In the beginning was the *Wisdom . . .*"[61]

In the beginning was the word, the womb and the wisdom and in their commingling, Great Mystery becomes (ehyeh) LIFE UNFOLDING MPV

---

[58] Mircea, Eliade, *From Primitives to Zen*, NY: Harper & Row, 97-98.
[59] Lewis Spence, 72.
[60] Stephanie Dalley, *Myths from Mesopotamia*, Oxford University Press, 1989, 329.
[61] Cynthia Bourgeault, *The Meaning of Mary Magdalene*, 176.

APPENDIX 1 – TSERUF

Abraham Abulafia, a mystic from the 1200s, was the founder of "prophetic kabbalism." He designed a chant based on the knowledge of the Tetragrammaton as a compilation of power syllables called a "meditation on the Name," or the practice of *tseruf*. Kabbalistic author Perle Epstein describes the practice as follows; the students would begin chanting: "At the appointed hour, the Abulafian Kabbalist began permutating the letters of the Tetragrammaton (YHVH) with each of the five vowel sounds until he had accomplished every combination of the twelve [sic] possibilities given him by the master. Rhythmically 'moving' them mentally throughout the centers of his body as he charted his breath and combining them with the other letters of the Hebrew alphabet, he began with *yod*, the letter representing the primal point in the premanifest world and the solid in the world of matter. The *hey*, second and fourth letter, stood for the breath of the spirit and a plane in the world of geometry; while the *vav* represented a line. His own head was fire, his belly water, and his heart air – the elements corresponding to the Tetragrammatic letters."[62]

Tseruf means alchemy or transformation. The idea is that by chanting these syllables, change will be activated. Vocalize each letter of the Tetragrammaton with one long exhale or separate each letter into 4 parts:

---

[62] Perle Epstein describes this chant in *Kabbalah, The Way of the Jewish Mystic*, Shambhala Press, 1978, 96.

Yaaa-Haaa-Vaaa-Haaa (pronunciation: The "a" sound is like the "ah" in ahhhhhh)

Yeee-Heee-Veee-Heee (pronunciation: The "e" sound is like the "ay" in "way")

Yiii-Hiii-Viii-Hiii (pronunciation: The "i" sound is like the "ee" in spleen)

Yooo-Hooo-Vooo-Hooo (pronunciation: The "o" sound is like the "oh" in "oh my")

Yuuu-Huuu-Vuuu-Huuu (pronunciation: The "u" sound is like the "oo'" in "oops")

To begin, repeat each line 3-4 times. As you get used to the chant, you can raise the number of repetitions.

Here are some ideas for experimenting: While doing the chanting, draw an image with your mind of a flame to represent the fire of *yod*. Yod is not only the 10th letter of the Hebrew *aleph-beit*, it is used in the formation of every other letter. It is the image of a small flame.

י

In your mind's eye, place this image of the flaming *yod* over your heart. Repeat the *tsuref* while envisioning the flaming *yod* over your solar plexus. Repeat the *tsuref*, envisioning the flame at your third eye.

This exercise can be continued, envisioning the flaming *yod* over each of the seven major chakras. Thank, bless, honor and love your experience.

APPENDIX 2 – TSELEM

So God created man in his own <u>image</u>,
in the <u>image</u> of God created he him;
Genesis 1:27

The word for image in this passage is *tselem*. As I wrote in Chapter 4, *tselem* is another multi-layered word that means more than just image. Here is my longer definition: *Tselem* encompasses a full-bodied, essential (as in essence) aspect filled with powerful divinely inspired vibration, directly from the source.

Three letters make up the word *tselem, Ts-L-M. Lam* or *lamed* (L) is the letter of expansiveness. M*em* (M) is the primal mother, along with Her element of water. *Tsad* (Ts) represents a person lying sideway.

Here is how the word looks in Semitic Early pictographic script:

ᴧᴧ ᴜ ᴧ
M L Ts

d'Olivet writes about the letter *tsad* or *Ts*: "This character . . .belongs to the hissing sound, and describes as onomatopoeia, all objects which have relations with the air and wind."[63]

---

[63] d'Olivet, 430-431. He continues, "Placed at the beginning of words it indicates the movement which carries toward the limit of which it is the sign."

The root of *tselem* is *Ts-L,* which means, according to Benner, "from the dark shadow of a deep place."[64] d'Olivet gives a more extensive definition: "This root . . . characterizes a thing whose effect is spread afar. This thing expresses, according to the genius of the Hebraic tongue, either noise, or shadow passing through air and void." He goes on to say that the *Ts-L* root is "every noise that is striking, clear, piercing like that of brass; every shadow carried, projected a great distance into space; every obscure depth, whose bottom is unknown: metaphorically a screaming voice."[65]

Put together as a whole, these letters describe the following: an expansiveness (*L*) of the waters (*M*) from whence humanity, or perhaps more accurately life/creation, emerges (*Ts*) and is enlivened by the element of vibration ("a screaming voice").

I don't believe we have a word in English that encompasses the depth of this spiritual concept. The traditional translation is "image," but the problem is that this word refers to external visuals without representing its essential core. "Image" implies that we may "look" like divinity, but our essence is separate. If we are created in the image of divinity, then divinity is "other" to ourselves and hence dualistic.

Such a separation makes it easy for people to anthropomorphize a god like Jehovah, to think of "him" as an old man with a white beard and a temper. It also makes it easier for we humans to separate ourselves from nature, take on an air of superiority and feel that we are the image of God (or creation) whereas, say, a flower or a cat would not be.

For these reasons, I feel that *reflection* is a closer, if still imperfect, translation of the *tselem* concept. If we are the reflection of divinity, then we embody the same essence, and hence are interpenetrated.

One definition of reflection given by the Merriam-Webster online dictionary is "something that shows the effect, existence, or

---

[64] Benner, 425.
[65] d'Olivet; 434.

character of something else."[66] Reflection gives a closer sense of "inner embodiment" or the belief behind inter-arching oneness. Leaf, dog, star, rock, human . . . all are reflections of divinity (creation).

Here is the rebus of the word *Ts-L-M*: a reflection of the Powers that emerge (ᴧ) and expand (ᴜ) from the abyss (Apsû) and the seas of creation (ᴡ) (Tehom) amidst great vibratory clamor. I note that a portion of the ancient glyph for the *reflection of Powers* (ᴧ) looks remarkably similar to the image of the seed on a vertical, manifest plane. In Semitic Early *tsad* resembles the letter *beit* whose glyph looks like a rising seed (ᴧ). In sum, *tselem* encompasses a full-bodied, essential (as in essence) aspect filled with powerful divinely inspired vibration, directly from the source.

APPENDIX 3 – LUZ

Luz [Strong's 3870] means almond. Why is the almond important? As with so many symbols, the meanings are multi-layered. There are two words used for the almond in the Bible: *shaqed* and *luz*. Below is the passage where God explains to Moses how to make a "lampstand," called a menorah, for the sanctuary. The menorah is made of almond blossom-shaped cups to hold the candles. The description is discussed in Exodus 25:31-35.

25:31 And thou shalt make a candlestick of pure gold: of beaten
work shall the candlestick be made: his shaft, and his branches,
his bowls, his knops, and his flowers, shall be of the same.
25:32 And six branches shall come out of the sides of it;
three branches of the candlestick out of the one side,
and three branches of the candlestick out of the other side:
25:33 Three bowls made like unto almonds, with a knop and a
flower in one branch; and three bowls made like almonds in the
other branch, with a knop and a flower:
so in the six branches that come out of the candlestick.
25: 34 And in the candlestick shall be four bowls made like unto
almonds, with their knops and their flowers.
25:35 And there shall be a knop under two branches of the same,
and a knop under two branches of the same, and a knop under

two branches of the same, according to the six branches that proceed out of the candlestick.
KJV

In this section, *shaqed* (Strong's 8246 and 8247) is used for almond. Almonds have spiritual significance which can be seen in this word usage. Strong's discusses its meaning as "divine watchfulness." Benner notes that *shaqed* represents an almond "from its shape like an open eye."[67] Brown, Driver Briggs, another compendium, adds that this is because it appears as if it is "early waking out of winter's sleep."[68] There are some who believe this can also mean who has awakened from a spiritual sleep.

The above passage expresses the symbolisms of the tree of life (in the form of the menorah) and the rising energies of wakefulness (the almond blossoms). It also includes the imagery of light via the candles.

There is another word for almond that is the name of the city where Jacob has his dream. *Luz* (Strong's 3869) which appears in Genesis 30:37. Luz is a native, wild almond.[69] *Luz* also means almond in Arabic and Syriac.[70]

The place where Jacob had his dream, witnessed the ladder and pronounced to be a "gateway" of divinity had been named "almond."

When practicing chants from this book, this story provides powerful images to visualize. From the almond to the light of divinity that both ascends and descends to Jacob's ladder which can also be seen as our own spinal cord.

---

[67] Benner, 465.
[68] *Brown, Driver, Briggs* #1052.
[69] http://www.bible-history.com/eastons/A/Almond/ Consulted February, 2014. "It is probable that luz denotes the wild almond, while *shaqed* denotes the cultivated variety."
[70] http://biblehub.com/commentaries/genesis/30-37.htm; Consulted February, 2014. In section "Treasury of Scripture Knowledge."

APPENDIX 4 – MYSTERY SCHOOLS

What is a mystery school? At its foundation it was an ancient school that guided students or initiates to study the great mysteries of life, particularly, why we live and why we die. It teaches us to define our "earthwalk." Arguably the most famous was the Eleusinian mystery school in Eleusis Greece.

We have firsthand accounts of those who personally participated in them, witnessed their rituals in public forums or interviewed people who experienced them. Here are the teachings in those writers' own words, preserved for us today across the bridges of time. These were written from c. 650 BCE[71] to c. 100 BCE[72].

For among the many excellent and
indeed divine institutions which your Athens has brought forth
and contributed to human life, none, in my opinion,
is better than those mysteries.
For by their means we have been
brought out of our barbarous
and savage mode of life and educated and refined to a state of
civilization; and as the rites are called "initiations," so in very
truth we have learned from them the beginnings of life, and have

---

[71] Homer wrote about the mysteries of Eleusis in c. 650 BCE.
[72] Sophocles lived in the 400s BCE and Cicero and Plutarch in the 100s BCE.

gained the power not only to live happily, but also to die with a
better hope.
Cicero Laws II xiv, 36[73]

Thrice happy are those of mortals, who having
seen those rites depart for Hades; for to them
alone is granted to have a true life there;
to the rest, all there is evil
Sophocles, Frag 719[74]

Beautiful indeed is the Mystery given us by the blessed
gods:
death is for mortals no longer an evil,
but a blessing.
Inscription found at Eleusis[75]

The soul at the point of death has the same experience as
those
who are being initiated in great mysteries.
Plutarch[76]

Even older, although far less known in the modern world, are the Egyptian mystery schools. According to Plato, Solon, a Greek statesman, met with Egyptian priests in the sixth century BCE. One of the priests said to Solon, "O Solon, Solon, you Greeks are never anything but children, and there is not an old man among you." When Solon asked what he meant, the priest answered, "I mean you are all young in mind."[77] In other words,

---

[73] http://www.san.beck.org/Eleusis-Intro.html consulted March 2013, quoted by Sanderson Beck in *The Divine Mother and the Veil of Death The Mysteries of Eleusis.* Cicero lived from 106-43 BCE.

[74] Mircea Eliade, *From Primitives to Zen*, 300.

[75] OpCit, /www.san.beck.org/

[76] Jeremy Naydler, *Shamanic Wisdom in the Pyramid Texts,* Inner Traditions, 2005, 54.

[77] quoted in Naydler, 40. The quote comes from Plato's Timateus.

the Egyptian mystery schools were considered ancient, at the time when the mystery schools of Greece were still developing.

There is even a tantalizing clue in the Bible that Moses, himself might have been influenced by the mystery school trainings.

And Moses was learned in all the wisdom of the Egyptians, and was mighty in words and in deeds.
Acts 7:22

We have no extant written descriptions of the Egyptian mystery schools but what we do have are their mythic stories and monuments that allow us to peek behind the curtain of their beliefs. Such stories hold the keys to looking at the processes behind their mystery schools. Mythic storytelling is also the key behind the mystery schools of Greece. The Greek templates were based on the folkloric life of Persephone and her journey to the underworld as a metaphor for facing death. These same processes also apply when one's life is upended such as serious illness, traumatic loss, etc . . A "death in life" as it were.

Just what is this underworld that too often shadows us at every turn? In mythology, it is a place. In psychology, it is a state of mind, a darkness of the soul. In our collective imagination, it is a hellish landscape that contains all our worst fears. In some religions, it is a place for punishment. In fairy tales, we might fall down a rabbit hole, be swept up in a tornado, or any number of other mishaps, before getting lost in a foreign land. Without warning, we can find ourselves in Oz, on Elm Street, wandering through Wonderland, or even approaching the fires of Mordor.

This is the questic nature of a trip to the underworld and the processes by which we endure, conquer, release, grow. In stories, it can involve the search for a sacred item – the holy grail, a golden fleece, the fountain of youth, a mystical sword, a cauldron of magic. These are all shamanic journeys that are also the foundation of mystery school teachings.

Many stories in the Bible are based on the same mystery school lessons.

There are five main tools that mystery schools used:

1) the labyrinth or spiral

2) water bathings or original baptisms

3) teachings of the seeds

4) mystery plays that also called passion plays. These plays are often told as tales in the form of a journey or a quest as is especially prominent in the King Arthur tales

5) Mythic storytelling, often involving the theme of a journey or a quest.

The Labyrinth

The Labyrinth is an age-old tool for spiritual teachings. It provides the opportunity for a firsthand experience of the life/death/rebirth mysteries. In older cultures, it was considered the birth canal of the Great Goddess. The trip the center was seen as a symbolic movement toward a death in life. Walking outwards as the journey to rebirth. From the most ancient designs to the floor of the Chartres Cathedral, it has been used for meditation, stress relief, spiritual growth, teachings and ceremony.

Less well known is that Egypt had labyrinths that were even more famous than their pyramids. The historian Herodotus described his enchantment with them when he visited one in the 5th century BCE. By the time he visited the site, it was at least 1300 years old. He wrote: "I visited this building and found it to surpass description; for if all the great works of the Greeks could be put together in one, they would not equal this Labyrinth. The Pyramids likewise surpass description, but the Labyrinth surpasses the Pyramids."[78]

---

[78] Quoted from http://amazeingart.com/seven-wonders/egyptian-labyrinth.html; Consulted 11/1/14. Greek geographer Strabo also visited it and described it in the 1st century BCE.

According to comparative literature professor Wendy B. Faris, Egypt had the "oldest known man-made labyrinth."[79] Pliny wrote that Daedalus took his knowledge from the Egyptians for the labyrinth he built in Crete.[80] Labyrinths from antiquity are widespread phenomena, found in such areas as the Mediterranean, northern Europe, and pre-Columbian America.[81]

Authors Anne Baring and Jules Cashford discuss their age-old lineage: "From the labyrinthine passages of the Palaeolithic caves to the labyrinth inscribed on the floor of Chartres Cathedral there is a distance of twenty-five millennia in linear time, but an identity of symbolic image that nullifies the passage of centuries."[82]

Others describe it as a "structure of initiation." Rene Guénon writes about it being a "spiritual centre" that is ultimately "every place of initiation." It corresponds to "the central point, which is, both macrocosmically as well as microcosmically, the point of communication with all the higher and lower states."[83]

The Taoist term for holy places is "cave heaven."[84] This would be an excellent description of the center of the labyrinth as a place of threshold where different worlds meet. This concept is seen in the building of many ancient temple sites where a stone temple sitting on the earth is accompanied by caves underneath. This is found at Machu Picchu, the feathered serpent temple at Teotihuacan, and the oracle site at Delphi.

Guénon takes the theme further in discussing apparently opposed aspects such as life and death. He writes that reconciling

---

[79] Jean-Charles Seigneuret, ed. *Dictionary of Literary Themes and Motifs*; Wendy B. Faris, *"Labyrinth"*; 691.

[80] Ibid.

[81] Ariel Golan, *Prehistoric Religion; Mythology, Symbolism*, 300-302.

[82] Anne Baring and Jules Cashford, *The Myth of the Goddess: Evolution of an Image*; 42.

[83] Rene Guénon, *Fundamental Symbols*, 144.

[84] Golan, *Prehistoric Religion,* 308.

them brings the awareness that they are simply two aspects of one changing state.[85]

Original Baptism

The rite of baptism, original baptism which is different than it is known today, has been a tool of mystery schools for as long as they have existed. As Russian occultist Madame Blavatsky notes its reach and breadth, "Baptism is one of the oldest rites and was practiced by all nations in their Mysteries, as sacred ablutions."[86]

The experience of a baptism fits into these same mythical themes that mystery schools specifically address, those of life/death/rebirth. As Christian author Marcus Borg writes, "Baptism, the early church's ritual of initiation, was understood as a death of an old self and a resurrection of a new self."[87] Inherent in the rite of bathing, an initiate would have a visceral, personal experience of death with immersion into the water and then rebirth by returning to light, air and breath.

We know that the tradition of bathing was practiced well into the era of Biblical history. In fact, water purification is practiced to this day. For the Hindus, who still bathe in the Ganges, it is said, "As fire consumes wood, so does Ganga consume sins."[88]

In the following passage from 2Kings, Naaman sought a cure for his leprosy. He was instructed to bath in the Jordan River. Since such a bathing ritual would not actually be a cure for leprosy, we can infer that the cleansing aspect of the bathing was a spiritual purification. That he emerged from the waters in a state of being "reborn like a child" ties his experience in with the ancient baptism rituals.

---

[85] Guénon, 140-141. He includes a footnote about mystery school teachings, saying that the process of reconciliation is reminiscent of the grain of wheat in the Eleusinian mysteries.
[86] Blavatsky, Helene Petrovna, *Isis Unveiled*, Volume 2, part 1;134.
[87] Marcus J. Borg, *Jesus: A New Vision,* 113.
[88] Quoted in Hans Biedermann, *Dictionary of Symbolism*, 285.

And Elisha sent a messenger unto him (Naaman), saying,
Go and wash in Jordan seven times,
and thy flesh shall come again to thee, and thou shalt be
clean . . .
Then went he down, and dipped himself seven times in
Jordan,
according to the saying of the man of God:
and his flesh came again like unto the flesh of a little
child, and he was clean.
2Kings 5:10 and 5:14

Christ himself experienced bathing as purification with his teacher John the Baptist in the River Jordan.

After Jesus was baptized,
He went up immediately from the water.
The heavens suddenly opened for Him and He saw the
Spirit of God descending like a dove
and coming down on Him
Matthew 3:16 (HCSB)

Where did John the Baptist learn his trade? The lineage for how to perform this rite had to have been handed down from some older, more ancient tradition. Even though there is no extant evidence that the neighboring Egyptians engaged in baptism rites, it's not too hard to see how that tradition could have flourished in that culture. Egypt had the primary tool necessary, the long banks of the Nile River, waters that were considered sacred. All along these banks there was a system of temples and initiation centers, all connected with the mysteries of Isis and Osiris.[89] These two gods' storied adventures in going to and from the underworld parallel the myths of Demeter and Persephone which underlie the Eleusinian mysteries. In other words, their temples were built as

---

[89] Temples such as Dendera, Kom Ombo and Karnak.

centers of teaching and initiation using the life/death/rebirth model.

There were also others who practiced this rite in Biblical times. The sect called the Essenes were known as regular practitioners of daily immersion. In the Talmud, these daily bathing practitioners are called *tovelei shaharit*, or "dawn bathers."[90] The practice of dawn bathing grew into the ceremony of a *mikveh*. The original *mikveh* bathing was done in Earth's "living waters" – a rapidly running river, or in the ocean itself. It was likely done in the pre-dawn hour, so that the initiate went into the water in the darkness of night and was reborn by emerging from the waters just as the dawn revealed the day's birthing light.

There is even a Jewish tradition of using the ocean for purification rites. Dr. Ron Mosely explains, "On the third day of creation we see the source of the word *mikveh* for the first time in Genesis 1:10 when the Lord says, '...to the gathering (*mikveh*) of waters, He called seas.' Because of this reference in Genesis the ocean is still a legitimate *mikveh*."[91]

Through the process, the initiate personally and consciously experiences the power of being reborn through the body of the Great Mother in her watery aspect.

Teachings of the Seeds

The schools had many teachings and tools to impart this lesson. Perhaps the best-known is the teaching of the "ear of wheat." The symbology of the seed of the wheat (or barley) follows along the same theme: the cycles of nature, and most specifically life/death/rebirth. The seed is both the beginning of life and its end.

------

[90] Ron Moseley, Ph.D *Mystical Mikveh Immersion,* /http://www.essene.com/B%27naiAmen/MysticalImmersion.htm/; consulted February 2013.
[91] Ron Moseley, Ph.D *The Jewish Background of Jewish Baptism*, originally appearing in *Tree of Life* magazine, /http://www.haydid.org/ronimmer.htm; consulted December 2012.

Here is the template: A seed in soil grows roots into the earth, sprouts into a plant and at the end of its life creates a new seed. This new seed needs to "die" off the living plant and fall into the dark, fertile earth in order to be reborn. The lesson for us humans is that life is cyclic, and our journey continues in many forms, before our earthwalk and afterwards.

This lesson was found in Egyptian texts as far back as 1700 BCE, repeated by Jesus in the New Testament, and by Hippolytus (3rd century Roman theologian) in relation to the Eleusinian mysteries.

Whether I live or die I am Osiris
I enter in and reappear through you . . .
The gods are living in me for I live and grow
in the corn that sustains the Honored Ones,
I cover the earth,
whether I live or die, I am Barley.
I am not destroyed
I have entered the Order (Cosmos).
Egyptian Coffin Text[92]

Verily, verily, I say unto you,
Except a kernel of wheat falls into the ground and die,
it abideth alone: but if it die, it bringeth forth much fruit.
John 12:24

The Phrygians, the Naasseene[93] *says,*
assert that God
is a fresh ear of cut-wheat, and following the

---

[92]Edward Malkowski, *The Spiritual Technology of Ancient Egypt*, Inner Traditions, 2007, 362-363. Excerpted from Coffin Text 330.
[93] Greek gnostic sect from ca. 100 CE.

Phrygians the Athenians, when they initiate in the
Eleusina exhibit in silence to the epoptai[94] *the mighty and*
marvellous (sic)and most complete epoptic mystery,
an ear of cut-wheat.
Hippolytus, Philosophoumena, v, 8[95]

The Passion Play

Experiencing a mystery play is a tried-and-true method used to expose initiates and questors to knowledge for them to experience not only with the mind, but with the heart. Like baptism and walking the labyrinth, the experience also teaches about issues of life/death/rebirth. The Greek story of Persephone traveling to the underworld is one such mystery play that was performed at the mystery school in Eleusis. The crux of the story lies in the fact that Persephone ate six pomegranate seeds while in the underworld. The result is the mythic foundation of the cycles of the seasons and its role in fertility.

Egypt, too, had its mystery plays, with the pharaoh at the lead. One, called the "Mystery Play of the Succession," deals with the themes of seeds, death, rebirth, and the nurturing of life.

Egyptologist Virginia Lee Davis describes a play where Horus and Seth vie for the throne of Osiris.[96] Seth had murdered Osiris, whose son Horus sought vengeance. Stage directions and descriptions specifically say to place barley on the floor, and to bring in male animals such as sheep and donkeys to trample the grain while the officiating priest beat the animals:

Though dead, Osiris is ruler of the
world beyond and is resurrected as the seed

---

[94] Eyewitness. Likely an initiate. Epoptai derives from a word meaning "secret."

[95] Eliade, *Primitives*; 301.

[96] Jules B. Billard, Editor, *Ancient Egypt Discovering its Splendors Pathways to the Gods* by Virginia Lee Davis; 158.

*that becomes grain, the river that floods, the
moon that waxes and wanes. . .*

*In the play, the pharaoh, portraying
Horus, tells the animals not to trample the
grain (a symbol of Osiris). The animals
disobey. (The grain, after all, has to be
threshed – sacrificed – if there is going to be
any food). Horus then symbolically beats the
animals and, says the script, "Horus speaks
to Osiris: 'I have beaten for you those who
have beaten you.'"*

*Near the end of the play, the
pharaoh passes out food. A stage direction in
the script says: "A loaf of bread; a jug of
beer." Thus does food and drink – both the
products of "sacrificed" grain – come from
the king – god to the people.*

Storytelling

After the first-hand accounts, it is through stories and
myths that we know the most about the mystery school teachings.
Mythic stories have both exoteric and esoteric elements. The
exoteric story is the one that is told in legends and story books. The
esoteric elements are the symbolic sometimes coded messages, the
hidden teachings, and the mystery teachings that underly the
stories. The myth of Persephone and Demeter is perhaps the most
well-known.

The exoteric story of Persephone tells the tale of how she was
kidnapped by Hades when she was a young girl playing in fields
of flowers. In a show of great intensity, the earth cracked open,
accompanied by a great roaring explosion. The earth itself
trembled; the heavens cried misty tears. In terrifying fashion,

Hades rose out of the abyss in a chariot driven by two spirited steeds. He plucked Persephone from her play and holding her tight, dove back into the great fissure. With a thunderous clap, it closed behind them.

The story continues with her mother, Demeter, furiously going to Zeus to threaten him. As the goddess of agriculture and grain, Demeter declared that she would not allow the crops to grow again until Persephone was returned to her. Winter descended, killing all the grain. People began to starve. Finally, Zeus's hand was forced, and he ordered Hades to return Persephone to her mother. When she returned, however, it was discovered that she had eaten six seeds of a pomegranate. The gods sat in council and determined that, due to the pomegranate seeds, Persephone would henceforth spend six months in the underworld with Hades and six months with her mother Demeter. The story is still told to this day, as the quintessential origin story of why we have seasons. When Persephone is in the underworld, Demeter withdraws and it is winter. When Persephone returns, the sun shines again, Demeter, too, reemerges and the grain and crops grow plentiful, spring.

The esoteric teachings of the Persephone story deal with her time in the underworld and how she learned to guide people through and out, thereby becoming its Queen. Notice the prominent theme of seeds (pomegranate in this case) which are a connection to the mystery school teachings where the initiates contemplate seeds as part of their training.

Mystery school teachings can be found in threads through the stories of the ancient patriarchs and matriarchs although their stories are not always as fully developed. Whether these connections are due to formal teachings in an official school or because they are part of the shamanic/spiritual indigenous experience, it is impossible to know. The two are identical as to teachings although the tools for learning may be different. In ancient times, the road between the early Habirus and Egypt was well worn. Abraham and Sara went into Egypt at a time of famine. Joseph was sold into slavery in Egypt eventually drawing his entire family there. Moses was born and raised in Egypt. Even in the New Testament, Mary and her infant Jesus sought sanctuary in Egypt. Since Egypt had the oldest known mysteries schools in antiquity, it makes sense that those who travelled there would be familiar with the teachings.

Some of the clues that indicate initiation in a mystery school include fertility, name changes, the ability to do magic, a quest, a transformation of some type. After leaving Egypt Abram and Sarai received new names, Abraham and Sara. Jacob became Israel. Sara grew fertile at an advanced age. Moses was known for his power when pitted against the magicians of Egypt. He also parted the Red Sea. Job experienced his own passion play.

There is a reason these stories have all stood the test of time and continue to capture our imaginations. It is because they speak so deeply to the human condition.

David Elkington puts it in the most poetic terms possible when he writes, "When speaking our everyday language, we use nuances of sound to intone and differentiate and to give a sense of mood. Divine language was used and imparted in similar ways, but differently in that evidence point to it being sung, and at particular frequencies, with all of the brain wave changes this involved."[97]

DIVINE LANGUAGE WAS SUNG! Singing is vibration at its most beautiful and powerful. That is the foundation of creation.

---

[97] David Elkington, The Ancient Language of Sacred Sound, Inner Traditions, 2021; pg 213.

COMPENDIUM OF CHANTS

Chapter 5

Ehyeh-asher-ehyeh
I AM

Chapter 6

Ay-lee beh-air ay-new-lah OR
Ay-lee
Beh-air
Ay-new-lah

Chapter 7

quadosh, quadosh, quadosh

Chapter 8

ay-den-nika tasha-queeem

Chapter 9

lib-be-ka br-ka
leeee-beh-kaahhh brrrrr-kaaahhhh

Chapter 10
Ets, Ets-ah, ets-eem,
Etzzzzzz, etz-ahhhhhhhhh, etz-eeeeeem

Chapter 11

Ha-adam ets hassadeh.
OR speak your own words of love.

Chapter 12

YaaaHaaaVaaaHaaa

Chapter 13

HA-LA-LU-YA   AH-LA-LU-YA,
HAL-LU-YA, HAL-LU-EL, HAL-LU-HU

Chapter 15

Hineni, I am here!

Chapter 16

Yare yar-ayyyy.

BIBLIOGRAPHY

Jan Assman, <u>Moses the Egyptian</u>, Harvard University Press, 1997.

Baring, Anne and Cashford, Jules, <u>The Myth of the Goddess, Evolution of an Image</u>, Penguin Books, 1993.

Benner, Jeff A, <u>Ancient Hebrew Lexicon of the Bible</u>, Virtualbookworm.com Publishing Inc, 2005.

Adele and Brettler, Marc Zvi, editors, <u>The Jewish Study Bible</u>, Oxford University Press, 2004.

Biedermann, Hans, <u>Dictionary of Symbolism; Cultural Icons and the Meanings Behind Them</u> (translated by James Hulbert), Meridian, 1994.

Billard, Jules B., Editor, <u>Ancient Egypt Discovering its Splendors</u>, National Geographic Society, 1978.

Borg, Marcus J., <u>Jesus: A New Vision</u>, HarperSanFrancisco, 1991.

Bourgeault, Cynthia, <u>The Meaning of Mary Magdalene</u> Shambala, 20120.

Dalley, Stephanie, <u>Myths from Mesopotamia</u>, Oxford University Press, 1989.

d'Olivet, Fabre, <u>The Hebraic Tongue Restored: And the True Meaning of the Hebrew Words Re-established and Proved by their Radical Analysis</u>, translated by Nayan Louise Redfield, Samuel Weiser, Inc. 1976 (first published in 1921).

Douglas-Klotz, Neil <u>Revelations of the Aramaic Jesus, The Hidden Teachings on Life & Death </u>(Hampton Roads Publishing Company, 2022.

Eliade, Mircea, <u>Rites and Symbols of Initiation: The Mysteries of Birth and Rebirth</u>, Harper and Row. Originally published in 1958, 1965 edition, translated by Willard R. Trask.

Eliade, Mircea, <u>Shamanism: Archaic Techniques of Ecstasy</u>, Princeton University Press, 1974.

Eliade, Mircea, <u>From Primitives to Zen</u>, translation by HD Griswold NY: Harper &Row, 1977.

Eliade, Mircea, <u> Patterns of Comparative Religion</u>, translation by Rosemary Sheed, University of Nebraska Press, 1996.\

Elkington, David, The Ancient Language of Sacred Sound, Inner Traditions 2021 (originally published in England under the title In The Name of the Gods, Green Man Press, 2001).

Epstein, Perle, <u>Kabbalah, The Way of the Jewish Mystic</u>, Shambhala Press, 1978.

Golan, Ariel, <u>Prehistoric Religion; Mythology, Symbolism</u>, Printed in Jerusalem, 2003.

Guénon, René, <u>Fundamental Symbols</u>, translated by Alvin Moore, Jr., Quinta Essentia, 1995, first published in 1962.

Hanson, Kenneth, <u>Kabbalah: The Untold Story of the Mystic Tradition</u>, Council Oak, 2004.

Hanson, Thor, <u>The Triumph of Seeds</u>, Basic Books, 2015.

Heline, Corine, <u>The Bible and The Tarot,</u> DeVorss Publications, 1969.

Trista Hendren, Editor (and others), <u>Just as I Am: Hymns Affirming the Divine Female – A Girl God Hermnal</u>, GirlGodBooks, 2021.

Jastrow, Morris, <u>Hebrew and Babylonian Traditions</u>, 2012 Forgotten Books (originally published by Schribner and Sons, 1914).

Khan, Hazrat Inayat, <u>The Music of Life</u>, Omega Publications, 1998.

King, Serge Kahili, <u>Urban Shaman</u>, Fireside, 1990.

Kligler, Jonathan, <u>Hineni</u>, Blue Thread Communications, 2013.

Malkowski, Edward F, <u>The Spiritual Technology of Ancient Egypt</u>, Inner Traditions, 2007.

Naydler, Jeremy, <u>Shamanic Wisdom in the Pyramid Texts</u>, Inner Traditions, 2005.

Pollack, Rachel <u>The Shining Tribe Tarot</u>, Weiser Books, latest publication, 2024.

Seigneuret, Jean-Charles, Editor, <u>Dictionary of Literary Themes and Motifs</u>, Greenwood Press, 1988.

Spence, Lewis, <u>Myths & Legends of Babylonia & Assyria</u>, Forgotten Books, 2012 (originally published NY Frederick A Stokes Company, 1916).

Winkler, Gershon, <u>Kabbalah 365</u>, Andrews McMeel Publishing, 2004.

WEBSITES

Digital sources

Blavatsky, Helene Petrovna, <u>Isis Unveiled</u>, Volume 2, part 1

Concordance: Strong's

Concordance: Brown, Driver, Briggs

Specific Websites

http://en.wikipedia.org/wiki/Hallelujah

http://www.merriam-webster.com/dictionary/reflection.

http://www.bible-history.com/eastons/A/Almond

http://biblehub.com/commentaries/genesis/30-37.htm; In section "Treasury of Scripture Knowledge."

http://www.san.beck.org/Eleusis-Intro.html, quoted by Sanderson Beck in *The Divine Mother and the Veil of Death The Mysteries of Eleusis.*

http://amazeingart.com/seven-wonders/egyptian-labyrinth.html.

Ron Moseley, Ph.D *Mystical Mikveh Immersion,* /http://www.essene.com/B%27naiAmen/MysticalImmersion.htm/ http://www.haydid.org/ronimmer.htm;

https://www.britannica.com/topic/Isis-Egyptian-goddess

https://www.etymonline.com/word/Rig%20veda

GRATITUDES

As with any endeavor of this magnitude I have stood on the shoulders of giants to complete this project. My first shout out is to Paul and Laura Lee Robear who are directors of the Cuyamungue Institute (also called the Cuya Institute). I found them through a circuitous route. They run an experiential program of ecstatic trance which is achieved through a ritual process of the holding of postures. The postures are left to us by our ancestors in the form of artifacts. They also do research involving altered states of consciousness, brain patterns, and other related topics.

In 2022, the Morgan Museum in NYC had an exhibit about Enheduanna, the Sumerian high priestess and writer from ca 2300 BCE. When I first went to the exhibit, I noticed that many of the statues of the period had their hands in the same position. (see Chapter 16). I returned to the exhibit with some spirit-minded friends, and we stood in front of those statues mimicking their posture. Everyone's experience was different, but everyone felt some kind heat and energy movement in their bodies while holding the pose. Everyone agreed that it activated our hands, heating them up for healing purposes. I wrote this experience up in a blogpost. One of the readers recommended that I check out the Cuyamungue Institute where they have studied this effect for 50 years. Under the direction of their founder, Dr. Felicitas Goodman, they have developed rituals surrounding this work that are very powerful. They include prayers, saging, "spirit talk," and drumming or rattling. I recommend their website.

https://www.cuyamungueinstitute.com/

I am especially honored that Paul Robear, director of the Cuyamungue Institute agreed to write the Foreword to this book.

In this book, I was inspired by their work and use the concept of ancestral postures in a slightly different manner than they do at the Institute. My ritualistic elements are different. I use mantras and mandalas to enhance the mudras.

I would also like to thank all my teachers and mentors who have guided me, friends who have shared their spirit journey with me, Xochitl Alvizo who trusted me to co-weave the website FAR with her. David Elkington for his wisdom and inspiration. The writers and contributors have taught me so much and have rocked my world. Thank you.

I also want to thank two awesome editors who agreed to work on this book: Alice Laby and J R Turek. They, along with the many readers of this book, have made it so much better. My thanks to all.

My first line reader is always my husband Marty who stands by me and supports my work in so many ways. I love you.

I will be putting up vocal memos on my website if you would like to hear some samples of how these chants can be done. /mysticpagan.com/

BIOGRAPHY: JANET RUDOLPH

"IT'S ALL ABOUT THE QUEST"

Janet Rudolph has walked the spirit path for over 30 years traveling to sacred sites around the world including Israel to do an Ulpan (Hebrew language studies while working on a Kibbutz), Giza in Egypt, Eleusis and Delphi in Greece, Avebury and Glastonbury in England, Brodgar in Scotland, Machu Picchu in Peru, and Teotihuacan in Mexico. Within these travels, she has participated in numerous shamanic rites and rituals, attended a mystery school based on the ancient Greek model, and studied with shamans around the world. Along the way she earned two shamanic initiations. The first as a shaman practitioner of the Divine Humanity pathway. The second ordination in 2016 was as an Alaka'i (a Hawaiian spiritual guide with Aloha International). Her books include *When Moses Was a Shaman, When Eve Was a Goddess,* and her recent autobiography, *Desperately Seeking Persephone.* In *Persephone,* subtitled, *The True Story of My Shamanic Journey Through the Underworld,* Rudolph describes her own personal quest which brought her from trauma through healing to joy. She co-edited *Asherah: Roots of the Mother Tree* from GirlGodBooks.

Her specialty is original Biblical translations based on ancient script and shamanic teachings. Rudolph writes wherever and whenever she can to express, heal, inform, challenge, startle and to expand love. She is a co-weaver and writer at /feminismandreligion.com/ You can also find her work at /mysticpagan.com/

THE KNOWER OF THE MYSTERY OF SOUND KNOWS THE MYSTERY OF THE WHOLE UNIVERSE.

HAZRAT INAYAT KHAN
THE MUSIC OF LIFE: THE INNER NATURE AND EFFECTS OF SOUND

Other Books by Janet Rudolph

When Eve Was a Goddess

The Bible as we know it today offers a message far different than in its earliest beginnings. What was once an oral tradition of earth-based spirituality has become codified, the original intent obscured by translation after translation. Take a shamanic quest to discover long-forgotten interpretations of some of the world's most influential tales and journeys. From the life-affirming tale of Noah to the mystery that is the Garden of Eden, you'll discover secrets that have been veiled for millennia. This is the Bible as it was meant to be - not the heavily edited, adapted text it has become. This is original knowledge unhindered by the intentions and motivations of translators and religious authorities.

When Moses Was a Shaman

The Bible is full of awe-inspiring magic while also serving to record some of history's most human stories. Its roots are steeped in the quintessential riddles surrounding life's origins and mysteries. *When Moses Was a Shaman* delves into Moses's most famous legends to unlock hidden shamanic knowledge. This book explores how the stories of Moses's life have had an indelible influence on modern-day human experience. Come to discover a radically new and inspiring take on some of the oldest tales of the Bible. Take a deep dive into some of the most breathtaking moments of Moses's life including: *The hidden mysteries of his early years *His mystical discovery of the Burning Bush *His thrilling life journeys across esoteric, otherworldly thresholds *The dramatic parting of the Sea of Reeds *His personal interactions with divinity *His connections with fire, serpents, seeds, Venus, and the moon

ONE GODS: The Mystic Pagan's Guide to the Bible

ONE GODS: The Mystic Pagan's Guide to the Bible is a shamanic exploration of the Bible's great journeys, struggles, quest, heroes, and heroines. Janet Rudolph's ground-breaking book is an extra-ordinary look at Biblical mysteries and mystery. In her telling, it was Eve's birthright to eat the fruit from the Tree of Life for it bears her name – Eve in Hebrew means life. Drawing on spiritual forensics, she traces the footsteps of legends such as Noah, Abraham, Sarah, Jacob and Moses across cultures and time. The enigmas of healing serpents, burning bushes, heavenly ladders and more are traced from the ancient mystery schools of Egypt and MesoAmerica to the standing stones of the Celts and beyond. The Bible is represented as a dynamic living document, guiding the reader in a quest to discover personal answers to age-old questions: Who am I? What is my personal relationship to divinity? Why am I alive? Why will I die? Unveiling new revelations from the Bible's earliest teachings, ONE GODS provides inspiration and knowledge as well as concrete tools for readers to embark upon, add a touch of magic to, and deep their own spiritual journeys.

Desperately Seeking Persephone

Desperately Seeking Persephone is a thrilling autobiography that includes explorations of mythic worlds, fantastic adventures, encounters with extraordinary people and the visitation of an archangel.

It begins as Rudolph sets out on a quest for healing after a childhood of abuse and sexual assault. Her travels reveal a vision of what's possible when seeking out the mysteries inherent in the world. This is the tale that could have been told if Indiana Jones had met Joseph Campbell.

Rudolph forges her own pathway out of trauma and depression by using the Greek Goddess Persephone's mythic trip to the Underworld as a map. Along the way, Rudolph earns two shamanic initiations, described in vivid detail.

The shamanic journey is ultimately about discovering wholeness and harmony; wholeness of self, of relationships, of interacting with the natural world. Through the craft of storytelling, Rudolph reveals esoteric spiritual tools and processes that form a primer of shaman-craft. This is a journey that is personal, global and accessible to all.

Desperately Seeking Persephone is a humorous, engaging heroic journey with surprising twists and universal appeal. The adventures themselves offer a template of healing for anyone looking for their own pathway out of darkness and suffering.

Asherah: Roots of the Mother Tree (anthology, as co-editor and contributor)

In these starless and shifting times, the relationship binding woman to tree lies between dream and memory. We have forgotten so much. Retreating within to unearth buried stories, rooted in nourishment, is a divine act. Contributors to this anthology have shared their vision, creativity and surreal imaginings, all glorious and beautiful, whether written, chanted or drawn.

Asherah's story exposes exploitation, including sexual and environmental. She is calling upon those of us who weep, when trees are cut down, to rekindle our allegiance to Mother Earth. Behind us is darkness. Ahead, if we take the right path, a new age of possibilities: pristine, joyful, peaceful, restorative.

Asherah: Roots of the Mother Tree revives this Ancient Goddess, bringing Her back to Her rightful place in mythology and empowering women to find Her within.